practicing the
tao te ching

Also by Solala Towler

Embarking on the Way: A Guide to Western Taoism

A Gathering of Cranes: Bringing the Tao to the West

Tales from the Tao: Inspirational Teachings from the Great Taoist Masters

Cha Dao: The Way of Tea

Chuang Tzu: The Inner Chapters

The Tao of Intimacy and Ecstasy

practicing the
tao te ching

81 Steps on the Way

Solala Towler

SOUNDS TRUE
BOULDER, COLORADO

Sounds True
Boulder, CO 80306

Published 2016

Cover design by Rachael Murray
Book design by Beth Skelley

Printed in Canada

Library of Congress Cataloging-in-Publication Data
Names: Towler, Solala, author.
Title: Practicing the Tao Te Ching : 81 steps on the way / Solala Towler.
Description: Boulder, CO : Sounds True, 2016.
Identifiers: LCCN 2015044684 | ISBN 9781622036035 (pbk.)
Subjects: LCSH: Laozi. Dao de jing. | Religious life—Taoism.
Classification: LCC BL1900.L36 T69 2016 | DDC 299.5/1482—dc23
LC record available at http://lccn.loc.gov/2015044684

EBook ISBN 978-1-62203-635-6

10 9 8 7 6 5 4 3 2 1

For my teacher, Hua-Ching Ni, who has guided my own journey toward Tao with humor, deep insight, and wisdom for more than two precious decades.

Contents

Foreword

was born in China at the beginning of the Sino-Japanese war, moving constantly for eight years throughout China to hide from the Japanese invasion. In spite of this, I was fortunate to have received a proper classical education, to be groomed and cultivated as the scholar in our traditional Chinese household. I still have the distinct recollection of memorizing the verses of *Tao Te Ching* in the dim candle-lit air-raid shelters. The Chinese classics, including Lao Tzu's teachings and *The 300 Poems of Tang Dynasty*, were my constant companions in my youth.

Although as a child I hardly understood the deeper meanings of those words, I simply loved the sound of them and enjoyed chanting those comforting mantras. Subconsciously, these seeds were planted in my brain and in my heart and soul, waiting to come into full bloom in my adult years.

I came to America in 1955 for my advanced education to become an architect, a dancer-choreographer, and a teacher in the arts. I was fortuitously recruited by mentor-friends Aldous Huxley, Alan Watts, and Joseph Campbell to be a teacher of Asian philosophy and Tai Ji as "Living Tao" at the newly established human-potential growth center, Esalen Institute, in Big Sur, California, in the mid-Sixties.

My life took a sudden shift from academia to experiential explorations into the East-West cultural-arts synthesis. I began digging deeper into the wellspring of my Chinese heritage and have continued to invest my learning and teaching in this lifelong endeavor of creative discovery all around the world.

In my first book, *Embrace Tiger, Return to Mountain,* a transcription of my verbatim teaching in the early years at Esalen Institute, a chapter was devoted to my attempt to translate the *Tao Te Ching.* Even then I fully realized how impossible the task would be. It had to be practiced, as a new and always renewed experience, to become a constant ritual for all devoted Tao students of life.

I have known Solala Towler as a friend and colleague for many years, and I respect and admire his sincere and solid stance as a lifelong student of Tao. I applaud him for acknowledging this lifelong study to be a practice, a daily ritual, the same way we practice Tai Ji and Qi Gong and how we observe and marvel at the always new, magical sunrises and sunsets in our creative lives.

To fully immerse oneself in this ancient language of *Tao Te Ching*, readers must realize that no translation can possibly do full justice to the metaphoric and poetic allusions of the succinctly selected symbols in these verses. They simply provide spaces and gaps for the reader to enter through their own experience and personal understanding at the time of reading and contemplating these words.

Solala understands this daunting task well, and he has valiantly plunged into this abyss to share with readers his personal "practice" in the learning of these eighty-one gems of Lao Tzu's poetics.

Enjoy and treasure this exciting and rewarding journey into Tao with him.

Chungliang Al Huang

Founder and President, Living Tao
Foundation, livingtao.org

Lan Ting Institute, Wu Yi Mountain,
China and Gold Beach, Oregon

Introduction

The great tradition of Tao is not a lifeless, historical record.
It is an accumulation of vital experience. I assure you that it
is not finished, sealed, and closed, but remains ever flexible
and open to new additions.

Hua-Ching Ni[1]

Many people think of the *Tao Te Ching* as a book of ancient Chinese philosophy. Others see it as a guide to becoming a good ruler of a country. In modern China, it has been translated into the social dialectic language of the Communist Party. Yet, when read by a seeker on the path of wisdom, Lao Tzu's text is a wonderful and precise guide to the process of becoming a sage or enlightened being, a *zhenren*. For spiritual aspirants, the *Tao Te Ching* is a manual on how to accomplish, within oneself, a high level of spiritual cultivation.

Each verse is a step along the journey toward wholeness and deep connection to Source or Tao. The word *Tao* means both a path and walking on that path—this path that is a pathless path. The first line of the *Tao Te Ching*—"*tao ke tao fei chang tao*"—is literally translated as, "Tao can be tao'd not eternal tao." It can also be translated as, "The Way that can be followed is not the eternal or long-lasting Way." So how can we follow this way that cannot be followed, in the worldly sense? It is by studying the teachings and doing the practices that Lao Tzu offers us that we are able to make our own track, our own path, our own inner journey.

There are many practices within the *Tao Te Ching*, but they are usually obscured—either translated incorrectly or simply not understood by the general reader. This version of Lao Tzu's book is for the student of self-cultivation who wishes to use Lao Tzu's ancient and revered teachings as a guide toward oneness with Tao. Notice I do not say "*the* Tao." That is because Tao is not a thing; it is an ever-evolving and ongoing *state of being*.

In Lao Tzu's time, around the sixth century BCE, there was nothing called "Taoism." Originally, people who followed Lao Tzu's teachings were just called the people of the secret formula.[2] This was an era when mystics and philosophers lived alone in China's mountains or else in towns and applied his teachings and practices to their lives. Taoism as a religion came about six hundred years later, when Zhang Daoling was "visited" by Lao Tzu and guided to create a religious form of Taoism called Tian Shi, or Heavenly Masters.

Even so, in its essence, Tao is still beyond religion. For twenty-five hundred years, these teachings have been followed by the hermit, philosopher, and artist. Taoism is a way of deep reflection and learning from nature, which is considered the greatest teacher. Followers of the Way studied the stars in the Heavens and the energy that lies deep within the Earth. They meditated upon the energy flow within their own bodies and mapped out the roads and pathways it travels. This has led, over time, to the development of many practices that are used today, such as Chinese medicine, *I Ching,* meditation, feng shui, *chi gong* (qigong), tai chi (*taiji*), internal alchemy, sexual cultivation, and astrology.

Many of these practices grew out of the wisdom of the man we know as Lao Tzu, yet that was not his given name—rather, it is an honorific title. *Lao* means "old," and *Tzu* means "master" or "sage." Interestingly, the written Chinese character for master, *tzu,* is the same as the one for *child.* So, while he is often called Old Master, we sometimes see his name translated as Old Boy or Old Child, which is appropriate given the perpetual innocence cultivated through the Way.

Legend has it that Lao Tzu wrote the *Tao Te Ching* in response to a request from one of his students. Lao Tzu was the head archivist at the royal library during China's Zhou dynasty. He was in charge of all the ancient scrolls of the kingdom and, by fulfilling his duties, reached a high level of wisdom. In this wisdom, he foresaw a time when society would crumble and the kingdom would be ravaged by war. Upon this realization, he hitched up a wagon to his favorite ox and set out for the farthest frontier.

As the sage journeyed west, a man named Yin Xi, who was in charge of the gate at the frontier post of Hangu, saw a purple cloud of light drifting toward him. Because of this, he knew that someone special was coming. Sure enough, several days later, Lao Tzu arrived. After eating a hearty meal together, Yin Xi begged Lao Tzu to leave behind his teachings to pass down to generations through the ages. Lao Tzu spent the night composing the eighty-one verses of the text we now know as the *Tao Te Ching*. Then he departed for the wilderness, never to be heard from again.

Now, twenty-five hundred years later, we have this small, invaluable text to guide us as we embark on our own journey to the wild lands, to Tao. *Practicing the Tao Te Ching* is designed as a path of eighty-one steps, one step for each of Lao Tzu's verses. They are signposts that give us vivid descriptions of what a self-realized person is. We can recognize these descriptions as attributes we would like to attain for ourselves. Each step brings us closer to understanding Tao and our place within it—closer to Source and realizing what the ancients called our "authentic self" or what Lao Tzu calls "the sage." He gives us many descriptions of the sage, and we are meant to take them to heart or, as the Chinese say, to heart-mind.

In each step of *Practicing the Tao Te Ching,* I offer three sections: my interpretation of the verse, an in-depth commentary, and a practice that is either directly indicated in the *Tao Te Ching* or drawn from other Taoist sources.

The verses, as they appear in this book, represent an interpretation of the *Tao Te Ching* that is based on my deep practice and study with living masters in the United States and China. This book is not a translation from classical Chinese. Instead, I went through the many versions of the *Tao Te Ching* on my shelf, including direct translations by Chinese scholars. Then, I compared them with what I have learned in my Taoist training over the past twenty-five years and decided on the clearest way to present each step, or chapter, as it pertains to self-cultivation.

In Taoism, spiritual work is compared to planting a garden. We plant the seeds of spiritual learning, and then we tend the garden, patiently, with a light hand and easy spirit. We don't hurry it along but allow it to grow and flourish on its own. In this way, our spiritual work becomes a form of self-cultivation.

My commentary draws upon other ancient texts, such as the *Chuang Tzu*—the second most important of the ancient Taoist teachers. I also rely on the first—and, for some, the most important—commentator on the *Tao Te Ching*, a fellow named Ho Shang Kung, who lived around 160 BCE. His translation and commentary have a more esoteric, internal, alchemical nature than most. The third source of reference is my own teacher, Hua-Ching Ni.

In *Practicing the Tao Te Ching*, my commentary has its roots in the studies and training I have received from my own teachers. In this way, the book offers a real flavor of the original text as it has been used for more than two thousand years.

My hope is that after reading this book, you will come away with a deeper understanding and appreciation for what Lao Tzu's work is meant to teach. These eighty-one short chapters contain so much wisdom that you can read and study them for many years, always seeing new and different levels of meaning. As you progress, you will begin to understand each chapter of Lao Tzu's work in a richer and more reflective way.

How to Use This Book

Studying this book can help you avoid many mistakes and help you keep from coming to the stage of exhaustion without having to draw your last deposit from the bank of your own resilient power.[3]
Hua-Ching Ni

How do we embark on our journey of self-cultivation, our journey back to Source, to Tao? It is usually best to begin at the beginning. As you'll see in Step 64, Lao Tzu teaches that the journey of a thousand miles begins with the first step. This first step is the most important one, as it is often the most difficult. It can be challenging to get out of the ruts in which we have put ourselves. As with exercise, just getting off the couch is usually the hardest part—so, this first step is most important.

I recommend reading each verse and trying to understand it on your own first. Many of the verses are self-explanatory. Others will take a little more time. Each one is short, despite being a distillation of many years of Lao Tzu's training and tradition. At Taoist temples in China, people not only study the *Tao Te Ching* but also chant it each morning. It is believed that just repeating the words can bring clarity and spiritual growth. Chanting or repeating the words is a powerful way to engage the verses.

Next, read and contemplate the commentary. As mentioned earlier, I have brought together material from several Taoist masters and teachers in order to make each chapter clear and easy to understand.

Then, read the practice. When you feel ready to engage it, be sure to closely follow my instructions. Many of the practices have physical or energetic aspects that need to be done precisely; others are to use whenever a particular situation arises; and some give guidance on how to live a life of balance and clarity.

Once you have read the entire book and attempted all the practices, you can reread passages and repeat exercises in whatever order you like. But remember, it is important to build a foundation in your understanding of Tao. Take your time and be sure you understand each verse, as well as the practice, before you leap to the next one. If you feel you must jump ahead, be sure to do so with balance and groundedness. Remember to take the way of *wu wei,* or noninterference, not overdoing or forcing. The path of Tao is slow and gradual; each step is as important as the one that precedes it and the one that follows.

Another way to work with the *Tao Te Ching* is to use it as a divination tool, as people have been doing for thousands of years. If you do engage it in this way, be sure to take a few moments before opening the book to allow your breathing to calm and your heart-mind to clear. If your mind is not clear, the message you receive will not be clear—just as it is impossible to see through turbulent water to the bottom of a pool, whereas still water can reveal what is in its depths. Ask for information from your guiding spirits, spirit helpers, or ancestral spirits and be open to receiving it in any form it appears. Try not to ask yes-or-no questions. As with the *I Ching,* you can say, "What would the outcome be if I did Plan A?" and then inquire again saying, "What if I did not do Plan A?" or "What would be the outcome of doing Plan B?"

You might want to find a step at "random" that you will work with for a day for more. Sit in stillness for a few moments. Then pick up the book, flip to a page, and see what it tells you. The information you receive in this way can be viewed as coming from your higher self, your spirit guides, or the ancient teachers of Tao who are here to help humble aspirants along the Way.

Although Lao Tzu taught long ago, the *Tao Te Ching* is considered a "living text." It was not written for just one era but is to be studied and reflected upon for generations of students of the Way. Lao Tzu's spirit comes through the pages of this book, as if we were sitting right in front of him, sipping tea, and listening to him speak. To truly understand this book, we need to apply it to our lives, both inner and outer. To make Lao Tzu's voice our own will take much practice and experimentation. To discover the truths that Lao Tzu shows us, we will need to make his vision our vision, his poetry our poetry, his ideas and experiences our ideas and experiences. We need to approach the *Tao Te Ching* as a wise and trusted friend.

It is also important that when we take our first step toward the Way, we are headed in the right direction. Modern life is so full of distraction that it is often difficult to focus our minds on anything of depth. Yet, depth of focus is what will propel our journey of self-discovery and liberation away from the world of distraction.

Once we know *where* to begin this first important step, *when* do we begin? The answer, of course, is right now, in this precious present moment. Waiting until we "have the time" will prevent us from ever setting out on our journey. All we really have is right now. The past is behind us, and the future is ahead of us; the past no longer exists, and the future has not come into existence. The here-and-now is where we are and the only thing that is real.

So, how are we to walk this pathless path, this Way that Lao Tzu says cannot be walked upon, yet is so important to travel? How can we take that first step in the direction of Tao? The rest of the book is my effort to answer just these questions.

---

1. Hua-Ching Ni, *The Gentle Path of Spiritual Progress* (Santa Monica, CA: SevenStar Communications, 1987), 95.
2. Hua-Ching Ni, *The Esoteric Tao Teh Ching* (Santa Monica, CA: SevenStar Communications, 1992), 105.
3. Hua-Ching Ni, *The Gentle Path of Spiritual Progress,* 95.

1

Tao that can be spoken
is not the true and eternal Tao.
Names that can be named
are not the true and eternal names.
Nonbeing is the origin of Heaven and Earth.
Being is the mother of the ten thousand beings (*wan wu*).
Therefore in the realm of *nonbeing* one can
see the mysterious source of all things.
In the realm of *being*
one can see the manifestations of Tao.
These two have the same origin
but are called by different names.
They are both mysterious and profound.
Mystery within mystery—
the gateway to all marvelous wonders.

The Commentary

We begin our journey with this all-important first step. At the very first line of the text, we are told that this journey we are on cannot be described, explained, codified, defined, or placed into any kind of box or be put into words. Once we try to put it into words, we lose it. Not only that, but the names contained herein are not the true and eternal names. Nothing about this journey can be described in conventional ways. There is no clear map to follow. This journey may be described more accurately as a pilgrimage or spiritual quest.

Of course, Lao Tzu gives us some directions, points us in a certain way, and offers us guidance on how to follow this mysterious and wondrous path. It is up to us alone to find our way through the brambles and byways, through the sometimes circuitous, often confusing path-way back to Source—what Lao Tzu, for want of a better term, calls Tao. At the same time, he establishes from the outset that we cannot force our experience of this journey into neat platitudes or definitions; he instead encourages us to remain open to the endless possibilities that we will be experiencing on this journey.

Another way to translate "name" (*ming*) is "distinctions." Chuang Tzu describes how humanity departed from Tao through an overreliance on making distinctions between things:

> The ancient achieved ones' knowledge was deep and profound. What do I mean by deep and profound? Their knowing reached back to before the time when there were distinctions between things. Later on came men who started making distinctions between things but did not give them names. Then they began to give them names but did not yet distinguish between right and wrong. Then when right and wrong appeared, Tao was lost.[1]

Nonbeing, which is beyond distinctions, is what creates Heaven and Earth. To the Chinese, Heaven (*tian*) is very different from the Christian idea. It is not some paradise where we go when we die if we are good. Rather it is the source of life and is therefore associated with the sun, which many peoples around the world see as the source of life.

When Heaven is paired with Earth (*di*), all life as we know it is created and then sustained. Together, they are the source and nourishment of all life, "the ten thousand beings." As Hua-Ching Ni says, "The universal divine energy is the root of all life. It is the root of my life and the root of your life. With this root people never die, but if you have been severed from this root, you are dead already."[2] This root or source, which originally comes from nonbeing, becomes manifest in the world of being, as do we.

In this way, nonbeing and being are two aspects of the same thing. If we look with the eye of nonbeing or nonduality, we can see and experience the Source, Tao. Then, if we look at things with the eye of being, we see the manifestations of Tao in the world around us.

This idea is also captured in the title of Lao Tzu's work. "Tao" is the origin, and "Te" is the manifestation of that origin. Nonbeing and being. Inherently, they are both mysterious. The term *xuan* means "mysterious," "dark," "remote." Its color is of Heaven or of the mountains seen from far away. Lao Tzu describes this quality of Tao and Te as a "mystery within mystery." This points to something unknowable or at least hard to grasp. Yet together they constitute a way through, a gateway to all wonders. As Chuang Tzu says, "Let us free ourselves from having to distinguish between being and nonbeing, or between right and wrong. Let us dwell instead in the boundless place and make it our home."[3]

How can we reach this place of boundlessness? How can we learn to trust what we don't see right before us? How can we find our way through a world of so many desires and delusions? How can we find our way home, to our true home, our eternal home, what Lao Tzu calls Tao?

One way is to trust in our inner vision. It can reveal things to us that our outer vision cannot. It is in spending time in the quiet and still places within us that we will get all the information and guidance we need. To do this we need to learn how to tune out the mindless chatter that takes up most of the space in our mind and being.

The Taoists believe that the mind resides in the heart. It is in stilling the heart that our mind reveals to us all the knowledge we inherently have. Repeatedly, Lao Tzu tells us to forget "book" knowledge and instead receive the knowledge that comes when we spend time looking and listening within. This is a special kind of insight that is developed through self-cultivation practice.

In self-cultivation, we will experience what Ho Shang Kung calls "the Heaven within another Heaven."[4] This is the gateway that leads to Tao. In the steps that follow, Lao Tzu shows us how to do this. It comes down to what we focus on, as what we focus on is often what we manifest and how we see the world and ourselves in it. Lao Tzu tells us that there is a way to birth two worlds at once. Not only that, but these worlds have the same origin and are truly one at source, as are we. Once we let go of our self-imposed limits and cultural baggage, we will be able to travel through that "gateway to all wonders."

But for now, in this first step, relax into your being and know that there is so much more *out* there and *in* there than you have likely been taught to believe.

THE PRACTICE   Developing Your Inner Vision

For the first practice in the book, we are told that if we practice seeing with only the eyes in our head, we will only see the manifestations of Tao. However, if we learn to see with the inner eye, we will see the original source of all manifestations. In this way, we can learn to see beyond or below what the world of form is showing us and look beneath to what is really going on. This can help give us perspective, an extremely important tool for living our lives with grace and flexibility.

- Sit on the edge of a chair or on a cushion; close your eyes. Breathing through your nose, allow your breathing to become slow and deep. Place the tip of your tongue on the roof of your mouth to connect two of the major energy channels of the body: the *du mai,* running up the back of your spine and over your head to your upper palate; and the *ren mai,* running down the front of your body. Bow your head slightly.

- Allow your attention to shift to the inner world. To do this, sit quietly, feeling your abdomen expand with every inhalation and contract with every exhalation.

- Now open your eyes, slightly, about halfway. Let the light slowly come into your eyes. Allow yourself to relax your gaze into "soft focus"—that is, not focused on anything. You can move your head around a little, looking at everything that surrounds you while keeping this soft focus. Continue to breathe slowly and deeply.

• After a while, close your eyes again and look within. Spend some time here with the formless form, the Source of all that you see, hear, and experience. Feel yourself as being one with this Source, a part of the eternal ongoing flow of being and nonbeing.

• Look at yourself and your life from "inside the ride," seeing everything with a bit of objectivity. When we lose this objectivity, we become caught up in the world of dualism and forget our place. This is the result of putting too much emphasis on the outside world and too little on the inside. The Taoist masters tell us that there needs to be a balance between inside and outside, between yin and yang—too much introspection can also cause problems.

• Practice this soft focus so you can use it in your life to come to a place of balance. With that balance comes peace and a harmony so deep that nothing life throws at you will cause real harm.

• When you are finished, bring your palms together and rub them briskly thirty-six times. (In Taoist practice we do many things in multiples of three; three is considered the most powerful number because it relates to the Three Treasures of *jing, chi,* and *shen,* or vital force, essence, and spirit.) Place your hands over your eyes and breathe in. The warmth of your palms (*lao gong*) will enter into your eyes. Then rub your palms up and down your face and over the top of your head, down the back of your head, and behind your ears, allowing them to come together in front of your heart. Rest in that position for a moment to conclude your practice session.

1. Solala Towler, *Chuang Tzu: The Inner Chapters* (London: Watkins Publishing, 2010), 34.
2. Hua-Ching Ni, *The Gentle Path of Spiritual Progress* (Santa Monica, CA: SevenStar Communications, 1987), 20.
3. Towler, *Chuang Tzu: The Inner Chapters,* 40.
4. Eduard Erkes, *Ho-Shang-Kung's Commentary on Lao-Tse* (Zurich: Artibus Asiae Publishers, 1950), 14.

2

Under Heaven everyone knows that the existence of beauty

depends on the existence of ugliness.

Everyone knows the capacity of kindness

depends on the existence of the unkind.

Existence and nothingness are mutually born,

difficult and easy complete each other,

long and short shape each other,

tall and short rest upon each other,

sound and silence harmonize each other,

before and after follow one another.

Because of this the sage

dwells in the world of nonaction (wu wei),

and practices teaching without speaking.

The ten thousand beings rise and fall

and she makes no claim on them.

She creates but does not possess them.

She works but does not take credit for it.

Because she does not take credit for her accomplishments,

they will last forever.

The Commentary

According to ancient Taoist thinkers, there is no absolute reality. The existence of everything in the universe is dependent on everything else in the universe. To draw on the original metaphor, yin and yang are the shady and sunny sides of the same hill. What might be small to one person is huge to another. What is hard for one person is easy for another. What is fast for one person is slow for another. On and on, this is true for all things in the multiverse of Tao.

We cannot judge one situation by our own absolute standard. What is true for you is only true for you, just as what is true for me is only true for me. None of us knows what anyone else is really thinking and experiencing. We cannot measure or even describe another's experience based on our own. The colors that we see, the sounds that we hear, the dreams that we dream come from our own interpretation of the world. Someone else would interpret them in an entirely different way. This is good, say the Taoists. This is natural. The world works this way. This is just the way Tao manifests in us, individually and collectively.

It is in our attachments that we get into trouble: to our own dreams, our own experiences of the world, our own opinions, our own need to be right and others to be wrong. Chuang Tzu offers us a way to work with these attachments when he says, "It is when we give up our personal views that we see things as they truly are."[1] Lao Tzu introduces us to an alternative way of being when he describes wu wei.

Wu wei, often translated as "doing nothing," means not *over*doing. It means not doing anything to an extreme, such as overeating or overexercising, which cause bellyache and exhaustion. It means doing just enough and no more. It means not doing anything against nature or against your own nature. It means using the least amount of energy to get the most done. It means not forcing, not exhausting yourself trying to *make* anything happen—whether a piece of art, a job, or even a relationship.

Wu wei is "learning to allow," letting things develop in their own way and in their own time. We are able to adapt and, like water, to take the shape of whatever circumstances we find ourselves in. Chuang Tzu says, "Let things unfold naturally and let your mind be free. Accept what you can't control and continue to nourish your internal spirit. That is best. You must be willing to act in accordance with your own destiny. Nothing is simpler than this and nothing is more difficult."[2] It is so difficult, because wu wei asks us to refrain from anything extra or beyond what is naturally suitable or adequate in any situation.

Lao Tzu uses this teaching throughout his writing. We will see many examples of how to apply this principle, as it is the mark of a sage, or what Taoists call zhenren—a self-realized person.

THE PRACTICE Warming Up Your Energy System

If our *chi* (lifeforce) is too weak or "stuck," we will be unhealthy and have no energy for deep spiritual practices. We do chi gong practice so that we can become stronger, clearer, and more balanced. Then we can go deep in our self-cultivation practices.

Here are a few exercises to warm up your energy system. They are great to do in the morning before a chi gong or tai chi practice. You can also do them after a long plane ride or anytime you want to get your energy moving to prevent or overcome stagnation—that feeling of your energy (chi) being stuck or stressed.

- Stand with your feet as wide apart as your shoulders. Take several very deep breaths, exhaling as fully as possible. This will help clean old air and carbon dioxide from your lungs.

- Swing your arms back and forth with closed fists. Gently hit your "gate of life," or *ming men*—a point in the center of your lower back—with one hand. With your other hand, gently hit your stomach, then reverse. Let the weight of your arms direct the motion, and hit firmly but not too hard.

- After doing this for several minutes, keep your fists closed as you hit your kidney area, in your lower back, with one hand and your lungs with the other, alternating hands so that you switch sides. Again, let the momentum of the swinging determine how hard you strike your body.

- Then, with closed fists, hit down your back along either side of your spine, beginning up as far as you can reach and then moving down to your lower back.

- With open hands, slap down the outside, or yang side, of your legs—all the way down to your ankles. Cross your hands over your feet and begin slapping up the inside, or yin side, of your legs, left hand on left leg and right hand on right leg.

- When you get to your groin, spend a few moments slapping along each side. This will stimulate the many lymph glands here.

- Slap up the sides of your ribs to your armpit and spend a moment slapping here to stimulate all the lymph glands here.

- Slap along the inside, or yin side, of your arms, down to your hands. Then turn your hands over and slap up the outside, or yang side, of your arms up to your shoulders. Switch to the opposite arm. Then slap your shoulders a moment to loosen them up.

- Now, rub your ears to stimulate the many acupuncture points here. Pull down gently on your earlobes.

- Do a moment of scalp massage on your head.

- Then do Beating the Heavenly Drum thirty-six times: Cup your palms over your ears, sealing them completely. Then flick your index finger over your middle finger along the base of your skull. This should make a booming sound inside your skull and will stimulate the brain fluid there. (This exercise can be done whenever you feel tired from too much studying or computer work. It is a great way to wake yourself up.)

- Now tap your teeth together thirty-six times. This will stimulate the flow of blood and chi throughout your gums and teeth.

- To finish, shake out your arms and legs and greet the day fresh.

---

1. Solala Towler, *Chuang Tzu: The Inner Chapters* (London: Watkins Publishing, 2010), 34.
2. Ibid.

3

Not praising the talented prevents jealousy.
Not storing up riches prevents stealing.
By not displaying valuable things
people's hearts are not troubled.
This is why sages empty their heart-minds
and fill their bellies (*dantian*).
They weaken their ambitions
and strengthen their bodies.
They are free of knowledge and desires.
By practicing not doing (wu wei)
they live in peace and inner harmony.

The Commentary

In this step, Lao Tzu tells us how to avoid pangs of jealousy over how much other people are accomplishing, which cause us to feel inferior. This step builds on the previous description of the sage as one who accomplishes, but does not become attached to his accomplishments. Ho Shang Kung says, "Do not contend for merit and glory but return to nature."[1] In today's consumer society, we are often judged by how much we produce or by how much we consume, yet if we consume or own too much, we become paranoid that someone will take things away.

The next part is an extremely important antidote to this and is usually mistranslated: it refers to the practice of meditation or "empty mind" practice. To Taoists, our mind resides in our heart. The written character for heart is *xin,* which is where both our cognitive mind and our *shen* (spirit) live. Shen is our spiritual energy as well as our creative energy and includes our thought processes. To "empty the mind" is one goal in stillness, or meditation, practice. Lao Tzu will return to this idea in later steps.

When Lao Tzu says "fill their bellies," he does not mean that the sage is constantly eating. Instead, it refers to the lower dantian. *Dantian*, which means "field of elixir" or "field of medicine," is where the internal alchemy practices called *nei dan* begin. There are three dantians: one in our lower abdomen called the Jade Pond, a little below our navel and a third of the way inside our body; the middle dantian, called Red Palace, is located in our heart center; and the upper dantian, called the Heavenly Center, is found in the center of our brain, or our third-eye point. The lower dantian is associated with the prostate or ovaries, while the middle dantian is associated with the thymus gland, and the upper dantian is associated with our pineal gland.

The lower dantian, referred to in this verse, is our body's energetic foundation. Just as a house needs a strong foundation, we need to build up our energy in this all-important center. The lower dantian is associated with the element water. So the "cooking" or "alchemic" practice described in this step involves putting the "fire" of the heart-mind down below the "water" of the lower dantian. The fire of the intellect, unless it is properly trained, will consume us with endless thoughts and thoughts about our thoughts and so on, leading to exhaustion or worse. The interaction of the fire (*li*) of the mind and the water (*kan*) of the lower dantian creates steam, or new chi. This is then further cultivated until it is transformed to pure spirit, or shen. From there, the cultivation practice is to transform shen back to *wuji*, or the "primordial origin," and ultimately to Tao.

THE PRACTICE   Filling the Jade Pond

By working with energetic practices like this one, our energy becomes increasingly subtle—ultimately leading to union with the subtle source of all life, Tao. Although our minds reside in our hearts, many thought processes leave us stuck in our heads. Energetically, we end up with gigantic heads and no bottom. In this practice, we are taking the fire of the mind and putting it under the water of the lower dantian. By putting our mind-intent here, our energy will naturally flow downward, and we will become more balanced.

- Sit quietly on the edge of a chair or on a cushion. Close your eyes and breathe slowly and deeply through your nose. Your breathing should be so light that a feather held in front of your nose would not move. This will take some time, so go slowly, without worry.

- With each inhalation, feel your lower dantian expand. On each exhalation, feel your lower abdomen contract. This is the type of breathing you did in the womb, when you were breathing through your navel.

- Put your mind-intent down into your lower abdomen. Don't try to *make* anything happen, just let the energy flow downward naturally. Eventually, you may feel some heat or tingling in this area, though that may not happen for some time. Just stay with the practice, and things will move when they are ready.

- For a healing effect, use your mind-intent to breathe in healing light on each inhale. Feel it entering your whole body, burrowing down to the dark places in your energetic or physical body, where any disease, pain, or toxicity exists.

- On each exhale, see all the disease, pain, or toxicity leaving your body through your nose as black smoke, dissipating into the air before you.

- Continue breathing in healing light or chi and exhaling black smoke. If you are suffering from disease or pain, you can gently guide the healing light or chi to that area, or you can just relax and let it find its own way. After a while, you will see the energy coming in as healing light and the energy going out as healing light.

- To finish, bring your palms together, rub them briskly thirty-six times, and then rub them up and down your face as you did in the practice for Step 1, Developing Your Inner Vision, on page 12.

---

1. Eduard Erkes, *Ho-Shang-Kung's Commentary on Lao-Tse* (Zurich: Artibus Asiae Publishers, 1950), 17.

4

Tao is an empty vessel;
it is used but never exhausted.
It is the fathomless source
of the ten thousand beings!
It blunts the sharp
and untangles the knots.
It softens the glare
and unites with the dust of the world.
It is tranquil and serene
and endures forever.
I do not know from where it comes
yet it is the ancestor of us all.

The Commentary

We now have a description of Tao and some of its attributes. It's empty, like an empty vessel; yet this vessel contains all there is. It can also be likened to chi gong and tai chi practices, which are described as "stillness within movement." The goal is to reach total internal stillness while moving. This is a high state of practice and can take years to achieve—or it can be achieved in a moment, if the practitioner is ready.

In the same way, stillness or meditation practice is described as "movement within stillness," because in the midst of utter stillness, within and without, internal forces will begin to move by themselves. The beginning stage of this practice is known as "mind (*yi*) leads the chi," meaning the vital energy will go where the mind flows. As you progress, the mind gets out of the way, the chi flows of its own accord, and movement happens naturally and spontaneously.

This step is the road map of our journey. It shows us what our origin is and the signs and wonders along the way. Lao Tzu tells us that when we empty our heart-mind of all the concepts and strategies that culture and personal history instill in us, we will be empty enough to be filled with Tao. Chuang Tzu says,

> Dwell in the empty chamber within, which is full of light. By dwelling in this stillness, great blessings will come your way. If you do not rest there, your mind will keep racing madly like a wild horse. But if you keep yourself centered and still, deep within this place, and allow your thinking mind to dwell outside, you will attract helpful spirits, and gods will come to your aid.[1]

THE PRACTICE Empty Vessel Meditation

You may be surprised at what you will receive in this practice. It may come in words; it may come as a feeling, a knowing, or an inspiration. Or you may just feel filled with something beyond words or description. It is a gift from Tao to you.

- Sit, stand, or lie down and begin breathing slowly and deeply into your lower dantian. Feel your entire lower abdomen expand with every breath, from the front, sides, and lower back. Do this until you feel very calm and centered.

- On each exhale, breathe out completely, emptying your lungs while your lower abdomen contracts as far as is comfortable. Inhale and then exhale completely, putting your focus on the out breath, feeling all the air in your lungs flowing out like air from a balloon.

- Feel yourself becoming more and more empty. Let all the thoughts, images, and emotions flow out of your body and psyche until you are an empty vessel. Allow your focus to soften and expand.

- Then just sit, with no expectations, no agenda, and no fear. Calmly abide in stillness, empty and ready to receive.

- You may find that you receive information or guidance at this time. If you think you will not remember it and want to write it down, do so quickly, without pausing to think about it. Then go back to the meditation.

- Once you feel you have come to the end of the session, end the meditation in the same way as in Step 1, by rubbing your palms together thirty-six times and then up and down your face.

---

1. Solala Towler, *Chuang Tzu: The Inner Chapters* (London: Watkins Publishing, 2010), 76.

5

Heaven and Earth are not benevolent.
They treat all beings as straw dogs.
The sage is not benevolent.
He treats all other beings as straw dogs.
The space between Heaven and Earth
is like a bellows.
It is empty yet never exhausted,
always in motion,
yet always producing more.
Fewer words are better than many.
It is best to abide in our true nature.

The Commentary

Heaven and Earth are not benevolent, says Lao Tzu, which might be shocking. But Tao is not a personalized, benevolent godhead smiling down on us from above, rewarding us for every good deed we do. It is up to us, individually, to practice self-cultivation and learn to follow the natural flow of Tao.

Straw dogs were used as sacrificial vessels in rain festivals and were burned as offerings. Lao Tzu is saying that Tao treats everyone, whether human or animal, in the same impartial way. Not only are Heaven and Earth impartial to all life but so too are sages. Sages don't teach people because of some altruistic idea but because that is just what sages do: they teach others.

On the journey of Tao, there is no one to pray to or supplicate or make promises to. Tao is very impersonal, but it is impersonal in the same way that nature is impersonal. Flowers don't really care whether we admire them. They bloom to attract bees and propagate themselves.

It is just life nurturing life. In the same way, when a hurricane strikes, it's not because of a need to destroy us; it's not God punishing us. The hurricane is just doing what it naturally does.

One of the main lessons from Taoism is that we can understand and experience just who we really are and live a life in the world doing just what we naturally do.

For many people, not having a personalized godhead is a very scary thing. If there is no big judge in the sky, looking down upon us and rewarding or punishing us, how are we to know what is right and wrong? How are we to know how to live moral and just lives? How will the bad guys be punished? In future steps, Lao Tzu addresses all this and more. But for now, we are left with a vision of Tao that shows no partiality to any living thing.

When Lao Tzu says that few words are better than many, he shows that he practices what he preaches. The *Tao Te Ching* is among the shortest spiritual works—perhaps that is why it has been so popular for so long. Each line is simple and even terse. He does not spell out everything. His map offers outlines and directions but not a lot of detail. It is up to us to fill in the topography that we will be traversing on our journey.

Ho Shang Kung is very practical when he says, "Much talking does harm to the body. If the mouth is open and the tongue protrudes, a misfortune is sure to happen. Cultivate and nourish the spirits of the five internal organs, save your breath, and talk little."[1] Over and over, we will encounter this advice. Yet when we come upon a new book, movie, piece of music, or even spiritual practice, we get excited, and it is difficult not to talk everyone's ear off about it. Sometimes others are willing to listen and sometimes not; we need to discern when to push forward (yang) and when to back off (yin).

When I first discovered Taoism, it was like coming home. Many people who have discovered the world of Taoist philosophy and practice feel this way as well; it feels so natural, comfortable, and right. We want to point out to our friends and family that, if they only follow the teachings of Tao, everything will be better—all their problems will disappear, their health will improve, and they will feel happier. Yet, both Lao Tzu and Ho Shang Kung caution us against talking too much and using too many words when a few will suffice. Don't try to be someone you're not. Don't try to parade your virtues and accomplishments to the world. Instead, stay true to your own simple, natural self.

While Lao Tzu says it is best to "abide in our true nature," at this point in the journey we may still be learning just what our true nature is! This is natural. Our true nature has been layered over by so much acculturation and personal history that it will take some time to remove these veils. As our journey progresses, the veils will naturally fall away, and we will shine forth as sages, as children of Tao.

There are several reasons that fewer words are always better than many. We lose a lot of chi through talking. By learning to speak directly and succinctly, we will preserve precious chi. We will also find ways to speak directly with simplicity, directly from one heart (xin) to another. This is a very advanced and powerful practice.

THE PRACTICE · Bellows Breathing

- Sit as before and breathe slowly and deeply into your lower dantian. Feel the movement of the inhalation and exhalation as a bellows that is keeping the fire of understanding and knowledge burning brightly.

- Empty your mind and just allow your breath to happen naturally, one breath following another, without effort. Another description of this breath work is "being breathed," because it is as if you are not the one doing the breathing. You are instead *being* breathed along with the continuing transformation of in breath (yin) and out breath (yang).

- Feel yourself as a living example of the famous yin/yang symbol, constantly moving, dancing between polarities. If you spend enough time practicing this state, you will carry this feeling into the rest of your life.

- When you are finished, rub your palms together as in Step 1 and then rub your face, slowly and gently, keeping your eyes closed until you are finished.

- When you do open your eyes, look around. Perhaps you will see the world in a new light, brightened by the fire of your inner wisdom.

---

1. Eduard Erkes, *Ho-Shang-Kung's Commentary on Lao-Tse* (Zurich: Artibus Asiae Publishers, 1950), 21.

6

The valley spirit does not die.

It is called the *primal mother.*

The doorway of the primal mother

is called the *root of Heaven and Earth.*

The valley spirit seems to endure without end.

Draw upon it,

it will never be exhausted.

The Commentary

Lao Tzu is describing Tao as the valley spirit. A valley is a place where the waters of life form a green, nourishing, growing space. This is a place that is below the forbidding mountains, where a river can trickle through, bringing life-giving waters to all beings. Further, Tao is not only a deep valley, it is the Great Mother, or *primal mother.* This can also be interpreted as "dark mare" or even "dark womb." The character for "primal" or "dark" is xuan, which can also be translated as "mysterious."

Most of the metaphors that Lao Tzu uses emphasize the yin, or feminine, nature of the universe. Later in the text (Step 28), he says, "Know the yang but embrace the yin." It is this mysterious feminine nature of Tao that the sage draws upon and dwells within. As Hua-Ching Ni says,

Every moment of our life is now pregnant with the next; we are all pregnant mothers in some way. The one who can control his life is the one who knows how to integrate himself with good energy to reform himself so that he is reborn in the next moment, and the next, and the next, continually following this way of life. This is cultivation of life, the Tao.[1]

Just like a pregnant mother, we need to nourish ourselves with good spiritual nutrition. We need to be careful about what goes into our energetic body and what comes out. We need to protect ourselves from toxic energy, and we need to get the right amount of movement and stillness.

Ho Shang Kung teaches that the doorway to the primal mother that Lao Tzu describes as "the root of Heaven and Earth" is the nose and the mouth. In our bodies, this is where the original breath, which penetrates Heaven and Earth, comes in and goes out. He instructs that our breath be slow, deep, and uninterrupted—in a mysterious way, "as if one does not exist."[2]

We will use this doorway breathing throughout this book and in our meditations and chi gong practices. By doing so, we will be able to connect with the root of Heaven and Earth. This allows chi to enter, gather, and move throughout our body in a smooth, free-flowing way.

In nei dan, or internal alchemy practice, we see the term *Red Baby* or *Golden Embryo* (*shengtai*). This is what is created at the highest stage of cultivation practice. It is birthing a new self.

THE PRACTICE Primal Mother Meditation

In the art of self-cultivation, we all become the primal mother, giving birth to our new selves.

- Sit or lie down quietly, breathing deeply and slowly. Feel yourself become filled with chi and spirit, as though you were pregnant with child.

- Envision yourself as a mother giving birth to a new version of yourself. (We all have an aspect of the Great Mother within us, even if we are male.)

- Welcome this new version of yourself with love. Feed it with your good intentions and your wish to become a strong, clarified, balanced person—spiritually, emotionally, physically.

- Ask yourself:

  What old, stale parts of you do you need to let go of in order to be born anew?

  What old patterns can you let go so your true self can shine through?

  How can you connect in a deep and real way to the primal mother of us all?

- Feel yourself as a mother giving birth, constantly and eternally. This is your Tao self, and it is as real as anything you can see in the world around you, if not more so. Allow yourself the time to really experience yourself as this primal mother, giving life and love to those around you, as well as to yourself.

- It is extremely important that you do not cut off these meditative and energetic states once you get up off your cushion. Keep them going throughout your day and throughout your life. Try to bring some of this experience of the primal mother into the rest of your life.

---

1. Hua-Ching Ni, *8,000 Years of Wisdom,* Volume II (Santa Monica, CA: SevenStar Communications, 1983), 5.
2. Eduard Erkes, *Ho-Shang-Kung's Commentary on Lao-Tse* (Zurich: Artibus Asiae Publishers, 1950), 22.

Heaven is eternal.
Earth is eternal.
The reason they are eternal
is because they do not live for themselves.
This is why they are eternal.
The sage places himself to the rear
yet always ends up at the front.
He is not concerned with his own safety
yet he always remains safe.
Is it not because he is selfless
that he is able to realize his true self?

The Commentary

Both Heaven and Earth are eternal because they do not live for them-selves. This step offers lessons the sage learns by observing and relating with this most basic natural state. In the following passage, Chuang Tzu tells us what a sage *is not*.

> Someone who has desire to have all knowledge is not
> a sage. A sage does not show partiality. The one who
> follows the timing of society is not a sage. But the one
> who seeks recognition and fame instead of following his
> own inner wisdom is not a sage. He who does not live his
> life guided by his own authentic nature is not a sage.[1]

The sage or self-realized one, on the other hand, does not strive to be at the head of the pack. In fact, sages prefer to lead from behind. Yet, by putting themselves at the back of the pack, they end up in a leadership position. The sage is also selfless. By not putting himself forward, by not worrying about his safety, by not calling attention to himself, the sage is able to realize his true self (zhenren).

This is what Chuang Tzu tells us a sage *is:*

> The ancient sages slept without dreaming and awoke
> without anxiety. Their food was not fancy and their
> breathing was deep. With this kind of person—their
> mind is free, their spirit is calm, and their brow is smooth.
> They are as cool as autumn yet as warm as spring. Their
> joy and anger happen naturally, like the four seasons.
> They are at harmony with all things and experience
> themselves as having no limitations.[2]

That phrase "no limitations" is key here. When we limit our expectations and ourselves, we limit our experience too. If we never dare to take chances and take up challenges, we can never truly know ourselves. Lao Tzu tells us the sage does not fear for his own safety and thereby always remains safe. "He thinks little of himself and always loves others," says Master Ho Shang Kung. Not only that but, "All the people love him like their father and mother. The spirits protect him like a little child."[3]

Taoists talk a lot about longevity and even immortality. Hua-Ching Ni tells us the reason ancient Taoists lived so long:

> The ancient Taoists would just be with things that were
> long-lived. For example, they would stay in a place with
> streams and mountains. Ancient people embraced all the
> long-lived things of the universe; they made friends with
> the sun and moon and all the stars. Their lives were so
> long, it is unimaginable to modern people.[4]

By slowing down, by practicing wu wei, and by identifying with long-lived beings such as trees, rivers, and mountains, we can perhaps experience a bit of the stillness and the wisdom of the natural world and find ourselves in harmony with all things. Chuang Tzu offers simple advice for how to get started by following the sages who "breathe from their heels." Most people breathe in a shallow way, "in their throats." The Taoist energy practices of tai chi, chi gong, and meditation all use deep, slow breathing as their foundation.

THE PRACTICE   Belly Breathing

When we are anxious, frightened, or shocked, we often find that our breath becomes constricted or even stops. By breathing in a shallow, fast way, we keep ourselves in a state of shock or "fight or flight" all the time. By learning to breathe properly, we can effect changes in our metabolism and even blood chemistry. It will calm us down, lift our spirit, and even change the way we breathe when we sleep.

You can do this practice whenever you are feeling tense or stressed. This is the foundational breathing practice that you will be returning to in later steps. Use the following practice to train yourself to breathe as a sage, "from the heels."

- Stand, sit on the edge of a chair or on a cushion, or even lie down. Make sure you are not wearing a belt or tight clothing that constricts your breath. Place the tip of your tongue on the roof of your mouth to connect the du mai and the ren mai.

- Breathe through your nose, slowly and deeply, allowing your abdomen to expand with every inhalation and contract with every exhalation. Do not overdo the expansion and contraction; instead, keep it nice and soft.

- Feel each breath coming into your nose and traveling down into your lungs and then all the way down to your lower dantian, in your lower abdomen. After a while, feel your abdomen expand and contract not only from the front but also to both sides and into your lower back.

- Feel your whole being expand and contract with each breath. If your energy is weak, pay attention to your long, slow in breaths. If you have a lot of tension or high blood pressure, pay more attention to your long, slow out breaths. With this practice, the slower and deeper you breathe, the more benefit you will receive from it.

- Do this breathing practice for ten to twenty minutes. By breathing this way regularly, you will change the way you breathe, even when you are sleeping.

---

1. Solala Towler, *Chuang Tzu: The Inner Chapters* (London: Watkins Publishing, 2010), 122.
2. Ibid., 121.
3. Eduard Erkes, *Ho-Shang-Kung's Commentary on Lao-Tse* (Zurich: Artibus Asiae Publishers, 1950), 23.
4. Hua-Ching Ni, *8,000 Years of Wisdom,* Volume II (Santa Monica, CA: SevenStar Communications, 1983), 8.

The highest sage is like water.

Water benefits the ten thousand beings

yet contends with no one.

It flows in places that people reject.

In this way it is close to Tao.

In her dwelling the sage values the Earth.

In her spirit she values

the qualities of a deep pool.

In her dealings with others

she values human kindness and benevolence.

In her speech she values truthfulness.

In leading others she values fairness and peace.

In serving others she values effectiveness.

In her actions she values proper timing.

Because she does not go against nature

she is free from blame.

The Commentary

Lao Tzu compares the sage to water, invoking the Watercourse Way, an important Taoist principle. Water benefits all, says Lao Tzu. Water from the sky produces mist and dew, and on the Earth it creates lakes and rivers. Water always flows downhill. It will gather in humble places like swamps that people often reject. It is in its humbleness and willingness to go wherever the flow takes it that water is most like Tao. Within the flow of water are shadows and reflections from the light above, yet it never loses its true nature. We can freeze it or boil it, and it will become different forms. But the molecular nature of water does not change. Can we become, in our nature, as flexible as water?

Water also takes on whatever shape it is put in. If it is put into a round pot, it becomes round. If it is put into a square container, it becomes square. This characteristic of water is also the mark of a true sage. If we can become completely free and able to flow with whatever situation we find ourselves in, we can live a long and happy life. If we are constantly fighting our life situation and trying to force it into the shape we prefer, we will suffer.

Not going against nature means not going against the natural flow of life. It can also mean not going against the natural flow of our own being. When we try to force ourselves into a shape that others demand of us, we end up becoming distorted and in pain. But if we allow ourselves to flow like water, we will be able to deal with any situation from an authentic place. By not going against the greater nature or against her own authentic self-nature, the sage is "free from blame." This means she does not suffer as others suffer; she does not distort her true nature in order to "fit in" with the world as so many of us do.

THE PRACTICE Water Meditation

- Sit, stand, or lie down. Close your eyes and begin breathing slowly and deeply into your lower dantian.

- Imagine yourself floating gently on the surface of a lake or a river. Feel the currents gliding gently around your body as you bob and float, at one with the water.

- See, in your mind's eye, the blue sky above you, with just a few clouds dancing along in the sky. Some of them may look like dragons, some like tigers, and some like other shapes.

- Feel the warm yang energy of the sun shining down on you, filling you with energy and light.

- Feel the cool yin energy of the water below and around you, holding you up and dancing gently with you. Feel how the water in your own body responds to the water below and around you. Feel the water in your veins and arteries speak to the water around you. Be the water being that you are.

- Let go, feeling your warm body blend easily and richly with the sun and the water.

- When your meditation is over, try to keep a little of that feeling of yourself as a water being: flexible and open, humble and adaptable. This will help you in your daily life and be of immense help in your spiritual cultivation.

9

Overfilling a vessel is not as good
as stopping before it is filled.
Oversharpen a blade and it will lose its edge.
Pile up gold and jade
and it will be impossible to guard it.
In going after rank and titles
in an arrogant and haughty way
you will bring about your own downfall.
Withdraw when the work is done.
This is the way of Tao.

The Commentary

This step is straightforward, in the commonsense way of Taoism, and gives us advice on living with the principle of wu wei. Overfilling a vessel leads to a loss of whatever we are filling it with and can create a big mess. This can refer to something physical, like water. It can also refer to experiences like emotions, thoughts, complaints, and desires—which, in themselves, are not problems until they swell to exceed our capacity to deal with them. Oversharpening a blade can refer to overthinking, to trying to use our minds to cut through our problems. If a blade, or mind, is oversharpened, it will easily lose its edge and end up worthless. The tighter our hold is on "gold and jade," or wealth and happiness, the more we become subject to "thieves"—negative thoughts, emotions, desires, and destructive activity—in our efforts to defend and obtain.

This is advice on not taking anything to an extreme. We think that if we are doing well in one way, we can carry it to an extreme and surely do even better; but often, the opposite happens and a mess results.

Lao Tzu tells us to do the work and then move on—don't stay around for the accolades and applause. We can do our best in whatever it is we do. And then we move on, *with* the changes rather than *against* them, because trying to hold back change for our own advantage is a useless endeavor.

Overdoing, overfilling, or oversharpening—all lead to failure. If we go against nature, whether the big Nature or the nature of our own being, we will run into problems. This haughty, arrogant attitude will bring about our own downfall. Ho Shang Kung tells us, "Desires hurt the spirits. Fullness of riches impedes the body."[1] Desires come in many ways. We can desire to gather gold and jade or we can desire to become enlightened. The most important questions to ask ourselves are: Do these desires help me or hurt me? Am I hurting others with my desires? Is my intense desire to become enlightened getting in the way of my becoming enlightened?

THE PRACTICE   Taoist Lifestyle Advice

Too much food, too much drink, or too much excitement—these can all harm the mind and body. Taoists teach moderation and balance in all things. If we apply the following lifestyle tips, our journey will be smoother, and our capacity to travel toward Tao will be enhanced.

- Eat only until you are 80 percent full, not 110 percent full! This way your digestive system will be able to work more smoothly and completely.

- Don't eat too much raw food, especially in the wintertime. Digestion is a process of cooking in the body, so too much raw food stresses the digestive organs.

- Try fasting one or two days a week as a twenty-four-hour fast. In other words, fast until the time you ate dinner the night before. This will give your digestive system a chance to rest. You will be amazed at how much energy this frees.

• Don't sit too long. Many of us work at jobs that require sitting for long periods of the day in front of a computer or at a phone. Get up and move a little between calls or computer projects. Stretching and walking, whether just around your workspace or outside, are all-important for the greater health of your body.

• Dancing is a great exercise that creates joy in your body and soul.

• Take time to dream and imagine and try something new—something that you have never eaten before, seen in person, or traveled to experience. It doesn't have to be a journey to a far-off land; it can be just around the corner or even a new place in your heart-mind.

• In hot weather, don't exert yourself too much. Doing so burns up your yang energy, which, in turn, creates an unbalanced yin energy.

• In cold weather, don't allow yourself to become chilled. Doing so will leave you open to "evil winds," or colds and flus.

• As Chuang Tzu says, "Blindness and deafness do not only afflict people physically; they also exist in the minds and attitudes of people."[2] Explore your blind and deaf spots to determine how they could open with a little work, a little sense of adventure, a little openness to change and transformation.

1. Eduard Erkes, *Ho-Shang-Kung's Commentary on Lao-Tse* (Zurich: Artibus Asiae Publishers, 1950), 25.
2. Solala Towler, *Chuang Tzu: The Inner Chapters* (London: Watkins Publishing, 2010), 9.

Can you hold the body (*po*)

and spirit (*hun*) as one?

Can you avoid their separation,

concentrating your chi

and becoming pliant?

Can you become like a

newborn baby?

Clearing your mind and

contemplating the profound,

can you remain unflawed?

In the opening and closing of the inner gates

can you take the role of the feminine (primal yin)?

Being open to and understanding all things

can you practice wu wei?

Can you grow the fruit without taking possession of it?

Can you do the work without taking credit?

Can you lead without dominating?

This is called *profound virtue* (Te).

The Commentary

The *hun* and the *po* are a very interesting and unique way of looking at the human soul. We are said to each have three hun, which are yang and are connected to spirit, consciousness, and the Heavenly realm. We also each have seven po, which are yin and connected to our lower, animal nature and the Earthly realm. One might also think of hun and po as our Heavenly self and our Earthly self, or our spirit and our mind. Many Taoist cultivation practices work to bring this mind and spirit into harmony.

Our po, or animal soul, is usually running the show. It wants what it wants when it wants it. This is what keeps us bound to the world of duality and to our various bodily needs and wants. It is what creates suffering in our lives. On the other hand, our hun, or spiritual self, wants to merge with the infinite and fly on the wings of light. At the time of death, the hun returns to the spiritual or celestial realm, and the po to the Earthly realm. In advanced practitioners, at death the hun and po do not separate but remain together. Within the Taoist understanding of reincarnation, this allows a practitioner to enter the next life with all of her spirits intact, which allows powerful cultivation to continue from one life into another.

As newborns, we are said to have our spiritual and animal souls in complete balance. It is only later in life that the animal soul becomes stronger, in response to the world we live in. Hua-Ching Ni says, "In the world the most powerful thing is the childlike heart."[1] Remember, Lao Tzu's name can mean "Old Child." The highest ideal of the Taoist sage is a return to the childlike nature of openness to the world, without any armor or fear.

After reminding us of this, Lao Tzu gives guidance on stillness or meditation practice. One kind of Taoist meditation is called *zuowang* or "sitting and forgetting." In this practice, we sit and breathe deeply and slowly and empty our mind. While it is impossible to completely turn off the "wild horse" of the mind, if we sit long enough and allow our brains to relax enough, we can cut down on our many extraneous thoughts. Then, once the mind has slowed down, we not only have a better perspective on our life, we also give our internal spirits the room to communicate with us more clearly. You can even call this another level of mind, or what Taoist teachers call "the mind within the mind."

Opening and closing the gates refers to the inhalation and exhalation of the breath during stillness practice. Our breath should be slow, deep, and silent, "so that our ears cannot hear it." This phrase can also refer to the changing of awareness from the outer world of form to the inner world of spirit. We can then take the role of the feminine, the valley spirit, the primal mother that we were to identify with and draw upon in Step 6.

Ho Shang Kung gives further instruction on stillness practice in this step when he says, "One must purify one's mind and let it become clear. If the mind stays in dark places [this is] the look that knows all doings. Therefore it is called the dark look."[2] This idea of the "dark look" refers to the xuan, or the mysterious aspect, of Tao. It also refers to keeping the eyes either completely closed or open just slightly during stillness practice.

The last line invokes Te in its highest form. While *Te* is usually translated as "virtue," to most Western readers that word implies a sense of morality—as in good deeds and treating others well. To the Chinese, and especially to the Taoists, the word *Te* means so much more. It can be translated in several ways.

One way is "spiritual power." Sages are people with strong Te. Their spiritual power has been developed and cultivated through their practices. Of course, they are people of good moral character, but in this case Te really points to a spiritual and energetic potency.

Another kind of Te is said to be particularly strong in places of great natural beauty, such as mountain vistas. This is why Taoists have traditionally cultivated themselves while living in the mountains. Te is also thought of as Tao becoming manifest in the material world. We can look at it as form and function. In this way, Tao can be seen as yin and Te as yang.

This step offers one of the most important practices in the *Tao Te Ching*. It plunges us into the practice of Guarding the One (*shouyi*). We are guided to bring the spirit and the body, or the hun and the po, together as one. This is no easy task as our body/mind, driven by our animal soul, is often run by various desires that can never be satisfied, no matter how many times we try to fulfill them.

THE PRACTICE Guarding the One Meditation

It is only when we can use our higher souls or higher selves (hun) to run things that these ever-increasing desire bodies (po) can relax and become less distracting. How do we do this? It is through stillness practice or meditation. This practice strengthens our ability to focus our minds in our daily life. It gives us the ability to cut through any mental entanglements, making it easier to process and make clear decisions about many things in life. Hua-Ching Ni says,

> It does not matter how long you meditate, effectiveness comes from constancy. Every day, wherever you have time available, collect yourself and put yourself inside of you before you make your next move.[3]

- In this practice, sit or lie down and focus on your deep, slow breathing. Close your eyes completely or halfway. It is important that you "shut the door of the senses," allowing no outside influences to affect you.

- Once you have settled down, focus your attention to the inside of your body, following your breath as your abdomen expands and contracts. Allow the many thoughts running in your mind to slow down and fall away.

- Allow your concentration to focus completely and deeply on Tao, the Oneness that transcends all duality and is, in fact, your true self. Keep your focus on the One, the source of all being and nonbeing. See beyond the world of duality, of yin/yang; see back to the Oneness or wuji.

- Do this for as long as you are able to hold your focus. In the beginning it will be a short time, perhaps only a few moments. But with practice you will be able to hold this concentration on the One for longer and longer. Eventually you will be able to drop down into this deep focus at will.

- As with most Taoist practices, length of practice is not as important as constancy of practice. But don't expect much benefit if you only practice a few minutes at a time. The rule for good results of a practice, be it meditation or chi gong, is a minimum of twenty minutes, which is the minimum amount of time for your mental and energetic body to relax enough to benefit from the practice.

1. Eduard Erkes, *Ho-Shang-Kung's Commentary on Lao-Tse* (Zurich: Artibus Asiae Publishers, 1950), 26.
2. Ibid.
3. Hua-Ching Ni, *Quest of Soul* (Santa Monica, CA: SevenStar Communications, 1989), 35.

11

Thirty spokes share the hub of the cart's wheel.
It is the space in the center that makes it useful.
When shaping clay into a vessel,
it is the empty space within
that makes it useful.
When cutting doors or windows
it is the empty space between
that makes them useful.
Benefit comes from what is there
while usefulness comes from what is not.

The Commentary

In ancient times, wheels had thirty spokes that all met in the center, which was an empty circle. It is the emptiness within the vessel, wheel, door, and window that makes these items useful. In other words, what is *not* there is what makes these things useful. Ho Shang Kung says, "Emptiness may thus make use of the spirits to receive all things."[1]

The Taoist term that is often translated as "empty" is *wuji,* which can also be translated as "primordial," "limitless," or "the origin of all being." In the first step of *Tao Te Ching,* Lao Tzu tells us that being and nonbeing have the same source. For many Taoists, that source is wuji.

Wuji, or the infinite, is invisible and can only be known through its effects. *Taiji* is "the world of manifestation." It is the perfect balance point between Great Yang and Great Yin. It is also called the Great Ultimate. It is thought of as the cosmic heart, as well as the human heart. In this way, our own small heart is connected with the Great Heart of the universe. When we are able to empty ourselves of our madly running thoughts and our thoughts about those thoughts, we are better able to connect with that great emptiness "and receive all things."

Dantian can be translated as "field of elixir" or "field of medicine." This is a very special kind of medicine, one that we create ourselves in our own body. There is a place within us, our dantian, that is empty yet full; it is a vast space that connects us to the vastness of the space outside of us. The more we consciously empty this space within us by limiting thoughts and worry, the vaster it becomes and the vaster we become.

The lower dantian is one of the most important power centers in our body. It can be found three fingers' width below the navel and one-third of the way inside the lower abdomen. Sometimes, this dantian is pictured as a cauldron, the kind used in alchemy experiments. It is associated with our kidney energy and our *jing,* or "essence." Kidney energy is associated with the element water; so the lower dantian is also associated with the element water.

The middle dantian is in the center of the chest, between the two nipples. This is also thought of as the heart center, which is associated with the element fire. The middle dantian is also the home of the shen, or spirit, as well as the mind and cognitive thought.

It is by putting our attention, or fire energy, down into and under our lower dantian, or water center, that true alchemy is created. Alchemy is seen as a sort of "cooking" process in which essence, or jing, is refined into chi, vital energy.

THE PRACTICE Alchemical Dantian Breathing

In this practice, we breathe and allow the fire of our heart-mind to descend to the water of our lower dantian. Then we empty our minds of thoughts, as well as we can, and allow ourselves to become empty, just like the empty vessel, waiting to be filled by wisdom, direction, and healing.

- Sit or lie down, as you did in the previous steps. Place the tip of your tongue on the roof of your mouth.

- Breathe slowly and deeply into your lower dantian. Sit quietly and place your attention into your lower abdomen.

- Let the fire of your mind settle beneath the water of your lower dantian and allow the water to bubble up until it becomes steam, or chi. Feel this chi flow upward as it fills your whole body with vital energy.

- Do this every day if you can. Slowly, over time, your dantian will become full of chi and your experience of yourself will expand.

- When you are finished with a session rub your palms together thirty-six times and then hold them over your eyes for a moment, drawing the warmth of your hands into your eyes. Then rub them up and down your face at least three times to end the session.

---

1. Eduard Erkes, *Ho-Shang-Kung's Commentary on Lao-Tse* (Zurich: Artibus Asiae Publishers, 1950), 29.

The five colors blind the eye.
The five tones deafen the ears.
The five flavors dull the palate.
Racing and chasing causes
our heart-mind to go mad.
Valuable and precious goods
hinder our actions.
This is why the sage cares
for his inner vision instead of
what he sees with his eyes.
He lets go of the second
and chooses the first.

The Commentary

Ho Shang Kung says, "Who strives greedily and lasciviously for beauty hurts the spirits and loses enlightenment."[1] Too many colors (sights) can blind the eyes, and too many tones (sounds) can deafen our ears, and too many flavors can cause our palate (taste buds) to become dull. When this happens, Ho Shang Kung says, "The heart is not able to listen to the sounds of soundlessness."[2]

Rushing after more experiences and more excitements will disturb our shen, and our heart-mind will "go mad." As previously mentioned, in Taoist practice the mind is said to reside in our heart—so what Westerners think of as psychological problems are seen as disturbed shen, or disturbed spirit. On the path of Tao, balance and harmony are extremely important, and anything that makes us lose balance and harmony is seen as destructive.

The sage is able to see what is truly real from what is only apparently real. He sees through the veils, through seductive but destructive influences, through even the world of manifestation, to see Tao. How does he do that? By using his inner vision and intuition, gained from his self-cultivation practices. He relies on what he sees with his inner eyes and lets go of what he sees with his outer eyes.

THE PRACTICE   Organ Balancing Meditation

Here is a simple exercise that helps develop our inner seeing ability. It also balances and tones all of the major organs in our bodies. In Taoist thought, each major organ has both a positive and a negative emotional tone. In this meditation practice, we emphasize the healing, positive side of each of the five major organs. In Chinese medicine, the organs are seen not just as their physical form but also as an *energetic* form. This is key to understanding the energy work in acupuncture, inner alchemy work, and medical chi gong.

- Sit, stand, or lie down and begin breathing slowly and deeply into the lower dantian.

- After you have settled down a bit, see in your mind's eye a cloud of energy hovering over your head. You can see it as a cloud of sparkling energy or just a cloud of healing chi.

- After a few moments, draw this energy down through your *bai hui* point at the top of your head (crown chakra) and down into your liver, which is under your right ribcage. The liver is associated with the element wood and with the negative emotion of anger. The positive emotion and energy of the liver is free-flowingness and flexibility. An unbalanced liver function means you will have a difficult time detoxifying your system; it can also lead to feelings of unresolved anger. Feel your liver energy soften and become more supple and flexible.

- See the energy cloud become a rich green, the green of new plants and of all growing things. Feel it envelop your liver and fill it with healing chi.

- Now bring the energy cloud up to your heart in the upper left side of your chest. Here the color turns red, the color of the sun at its hottest. The element associated with the heart is fire, the fire of joy, expansiveness, and creativity. Unbalanced heart energy will result in hysteria, so here we are emphasizing the positive qualities of joy and expansiveness.

- Feel the red cloud envelop your heart, filling it with healing energy.

- Now see the energy cloud moving down to your spleen area in your lower left side.

- Here it becomes a deep, Earthy yellow. The element associated with the spleen is Earth. It is here we feel our deep connection to the Earth and to all other life forms: the ten thousand beings. Unbalanced spleen energy will result in a condition of ungroundedness and worry or self-absorption. But here we emphasize the qualities of being grounded and connected to the Earth and all other life forms on our beloved planet.

- Feel the yellow cloud envelop your spleen and stomach area with healing chi.

- Now see the energy cloud move up to your lungs in your upper chest. Here the cloud becomes white, the color associated with the lungs. The element associated with the lungs is metal or, as in the ancient Taoist texts, gold. An unbalanced lung energy will result in a feeling of deep grief.

Our lungs are also associated with courage and the ability to surrender deeply to each moment.

• Feel your lungs enveloped by the healing white light.

• Lastly, see the energy cloud move down to your lower back to your kidneys and adrenals, where it becomes a deep blue or even black. The element associated with the kidneys is water. An unbalanced kidney energy will result in unfounded fear and panic attacks. But here we are emphasizing the qualities of "backbone" or "willpower" and of inner strength.

• Feel your kidneys become enveloped in the healing energy.

Spend time on each organ, really seeing the color of each. Allow the healing chi of each color to strengthen and balance each organ. By developing your inner vision, you will also be able to tell when one part of your organ system is weak or diseased and address it before it becomes a serious problem.

---

1. Eduard Erkes, *Ho-Shang-Kung's Commentary on Lao-Tse* (Zurich: Artibus Asiae Publishers, 1950), 30.
2. Ibid.

13

Honor and disgrace are related.

Accept misfortune as a part of life.

How are honor and disgrace related?

Upon receiving honor we become frightened

that we may lose it.

Therefore they are related.

Why is it that honor and disgrace both frighten us?

Why must we accept misfortune as a part of life?

Because when we have a limited sense of self

we experience misfortune.

If we did not have a limited sense of self

how would we experience misfortune?

Those who value their own well-being

equally with the rest of the world

can be trusted with the world.

Those who love their life

as if it were the whole world

will be trusted with all things under Heaven.

The Commentary

Honor and disgrace are usually thought of as opposites. But they are related because, as Lao Tzu says, when we receive recognition or experience success, we are so thrilled that we become fearful it will be taken away. This hinders enjoyment of the success and prevents us from building on it to achieve even greater success.

Taoists recognize that life is full of misfortune. Lao Tzu says we suffer because we have a limited sense of self—our experience of life begins and ends with our individual physical and mental body. But if we allow our sense of self to expand, we can have a sense of "the big picture," which would thereby decrease our suffering.

When we stop identifying with only our own limited being and instead expand our sense of self to include the ten thousand beings, we will attain a much higher level of being and living, because we know that we are all one great living organism. In this way we will be connected to and trusted by all living beings under Heaven.

THE PRACTICE   Expansion Meditation

How can we experience ourselves as not bound by our own limited sense of self? Here is a Taoist meditation—a visualization practice—that will help us take the first step.

Take time to feel each expansion, so it is a real thing happening within your energy body. Know that your true self is not bound by your physical body—your energy body is much larger and more expansive.

- Stand, sit, or lie down. Begin breathing slowly and deeply into your lower dantian.

- Feel your sense of self, your energetic body, expand three inches beyond your physical body. (Go slowly and really feel each level of expansion.)

- Then, as you breathe slowly and deeply, allow your sense of yourself to expand a little more until it fills the room you are in.

- After a while, expand even further to fill the whole building you are in.

- Then, expand to fill the city block you are on.

- Next, fill the whole town you live in, then the whole country, then the whole continent, then the whole planet Earth.

- Expand your sense of self until you feel like a giant planet, swirling slowly through space. Really feel yourself as a vast being, containing all the life that lives within you.

- You can then expand even further into space, if you like. With a little training, your energy can go as far as your mind can reach.

- After a time, begin to contract your energy body. Slowly become smaller and smaller, down through all the same layers you expanded into, until you are once again the size of your physical body.

- Hold the feeling of being a vast being in your memory, for you truly are that vast.

We suffer when we are stuck in experiencing ourselves as merely the size of our physical shell. By knowing we can expand and contract and can take different forms, we no longer suffer.

14

Look at it and it is not seen;
it is called *formless*.
Listen to it and it is not heard;
it is called *soundless*.
Try to grasp it and it cannot be held;
it is called *intangible*.
These three are impossible to understand
and so they are joined together.
The surface is not bright.
The bottom is not dark.
It cannot be held or named.
It returns to the origin (wuji).
It is called *the formless form,*
the image of the imageless.
It is vague and indistinct.
Looking at it,
its beginning cannot be seen,
its ending cannot be followed.
Hold fast to the ancient way of Tao
flow with the here and now.
Knowing the ancient beginning of things
is to know the essence of Tao.

The Commentary

Lao Tzu is once again attempting to use words to describe something beyond language. Tao cannot be seen, heard, or grasped with the literal or rational mind. We are reminded repeatedly that trying to use our intellect to understand Tao is not only difficult, but it actually takes us away from Tao.

Because Tao is the formless form and the image of the imageless, we simply cannot understand its true form by comparing it with anything our minds can understand. Lao Tzu uses language to go beyond language, thereby forcing us to go beyond thought so we can taste the true flavor of Tao.

Doing this is important, because if our mind is stronger than our spirit, we will be crippled. If our mind is filled with ongoing negative or self-defeating thoughts about the world or ourselves, this will also cripple our spirit. We must feed our spirit with good thoughts and good feelings. Otherwise, it will end up starving. Impoverished, our spirit will shrink and shrivel. Most of us in modern times have disconnected our mind from our heart. We do one thing while thinking about something else, resulting in a fragmentation and loss of chi.

Because Tao is vague and indistinct, the only way we can understand it is to follow the ancient teachings of the masters. If we can experience what they teach, we will indeed get to taste the essence of Tao. Ho Shang Kung describes this process like this: "To be able to know the beginning of antiquity is called Tao's Thread."[1]

We just need to connect to the thread. Yet how can we get beyond our limited, intellectual minds? How can we, immersed in the world of form, experience the world of the formless? One way is by connecting our mind with our heart so they are one.

THE PRACTICE   Embracing the One

The practice of deep relaxation allows the discriminating mind of duality to let go and allows the thread of Tao to connect our higher and lower selves into one harmonious whole. This practice guides our attention into our heart center. It helps align our heart with our mind so they can work as one unit.

While doing this practice, we may receive guidance from our higher self, our Tao nature, or our guiding sprits. These spirits are always with us, in our body. But because we are not aware of them, we do not hear their wise words of advice and inspiration. Call them forward and listen to them closely.

- Sit or lie down and close your eyes. Place the tip of your tongue on the roof of your mouth and begin breathing slowly and deeply in to your lower dantian. Spend a few moments doing this, focusing your mind on the inflow and outflow of your breath, the expanding and the contracting of your lower abdomen.

- When you feel ready, bring your focus up to your middle dantian, in your heart center, between your two nipples. Keep noticing expansion and contraction around your heart.

- As you sit and breathe in this way, let all thoughts go. Or replace the myriad, random thoughts with one thought of unity and harmony, which balances your jing, chi, and shen. Concentrate on this feeling of balancing your heart and mind. Do this until they work together, without space between them, so that your mind is clear, focused, peaceful, and relaxed.

- Feel all the extraneous thoughts, whirling round each other like wild horses, relax and let go. Allow your negative thoughts to float away like seeds in the breeze. Allow your myriad thoughts, opinions, and judgments to melt away like snow on a warm spring day.

- As you sit and breathe into your heart center, allow your heart to relax and, in that relaxing, to expand. Feel this heart energy expand until it fills your whole being.

- Finally, allow your mind, heart, and spirit to align into one. The ancient masters call this Embracing the One.

- When you are finished, rub your palms together thirty-six times, rub your face up and down at least three times, and then make a deep bow from your heart to the heart of the world, the heart of Tao.

---

1. Eduard Erkes, *Ho-Shang-Kung's Commentary on Lao-Tse* (Zurich: Artibus Asiae Publishers, 1950), 35.

15

The ancient sages

were masters at penetrating the subtle and profound Tao.

They were so deep that we cannot describe them.

They were cautious, like someone fording a frozen river.

They were vigilant, like someone who is surrounded by enemies.

They were courteous, like dignified guests.

They were ephemeral, like melting ice.

They were simple, like the uncarved block (*pu*).

They were open and wide, like a valley.

They were deep, like swirling water.

Who can remain still and quiet while the mud settles?

Who can remain calm and still until it is time to move?

Followers of Tao do not seek excess.

Because they do not seek excess,

they can grow old

yet constantly be renewed.

The Commentary

Here we receive a perfect description of the ancient sages or self-realized beings. After describing their qualities, Lao Tzu gives us valuable advice on meditation. We are often given the image of muddy water to illustrate our typical, day-to-day mind. It is only by quieting our body, energy, and thoughts that this muddy water will settle, with the impure elements sinking to the bottom, leaving pure, clear water above. This is the state of mind that can perceive Tao.

By not seeking excess, by not overextending themselves, sages are able to grow old in body but are ever renewed in spirit and mind. This is what Taoists call Forever Young, or *qing chun chang zhu*.

Breath is the doorway from one world to another, from our experience of ourselves as physical beings to our experience of ourselves as spiritual, energetic beings. Think of your breath as a door opening and closing. This door leads to a world of greater relaxation, insight, and healing. As we sit and simply breathe, sediment-like thoughts and feelings settle, allowing our being to become clear and pure, like a pristine lake.

Once this happens, our thought processes become nothing more than illusions—and even traps—we set for ourselves. As our being becomes ever more clear and pure, we may at last see and discover parts of ourselves we did not know were there.

THE PRACTICE   Stillness and Movement

- Sit or lie down and slow your breathing until it is barely noticeable.

- Notice how your mind and heart feel, or even look, like muddy water. This water is full of the impurities of self-defeating thoughts and clouded by ignorance of them. The water is impossible to see through because it is churning around and around in a whirlpool of worry and self-absorption.

- Sit quietly and witness this, breathing slowly, deeply, and gently—not forcing or trying to make something happen. Just breathe. Simply sit with yourself in whatever state you are presently in.

- When you have spent enough time in stillness, you will know when it is time to move. The stillness practice will feel complete.

- Slowly rise to your feet and begin moving, whether doing a tai chi or chi gong form or a kind of formless, improvised dance. It doesn't matter what the movements are; what is important is that you retain your feeling of deep stillness in the midst of moving. Stay in touch with the still part of yourself so that you are flowing like a clear, pure stream.

- After a time, allow your movement to become still again; either sit back down or stand with your eyes closed and your spirit light.

- Feel how the movement and the stillness were one, not two.

- Imagine how your life might unfold if you were to move through your days with this feeling of stillness within your movement.

- See yourself taking some time in the midst of activity to experience the movement of chi, spirit, and delight as it flows through your body and mind throughout the day.

- Experience yourself as a perfectly balanced, living, yin/yang being, at home in your body, your energy system, and the world around you.

16

Allow yourself to become empty.

Abide in stillness.

The ten thousand beings rise and flourish

while the sage watches their return.

Though all beings exist in profusion

they all end up returning to their source.

Returning to their source is called *tranquility.*

This is called *returning to original nature.*

Original nature is called *constant renewal.*

To understand constant renewal is called *illumination.*

To not understand constant renewal is to invite disaster.

To know the unchanging is to be enlightened.

To embrace the eternal is to be all-encompassing.

To be all-encompassing leads to nobility of spirit.

To be noble of spirit is to unite with Heaven.

To unite with Heaven leads to union with Tao.

To attain union with Tao leads to immortality,

living eternally without fear.

The Commentary

By abiding in stillness, in both body and mind, the practitioner is able to observe the world around her without being caught up in it. Ho Shang Kung says this step teaches us "how to return to the root."[1]

Because all things are born into being only to return to nonbeing, or their source, they "return to the root." Lao Tzu calls this returning to Source "tranquility" (jing), as jing can also indicate peace or harmony. This state describes how things return to their original nature so that they can experience constant renewal. To try to go against this constant renewal only invites disaster. At the same time, the sage identifies with the unchanging root of nonbeing, thereby becoming an enlightened being, a zhenren.

The goal of the self-cultivator is to experience this union with Source, or Tao, and become one with everlasting life to attain immortality. This reabsorption into the everlasting form of life is the ultimate destiny (ming) of us all.

This step refers to the practice of zuowang, or stillness meditation, the aim of which is to refine our thoughts. Other definitions of zuowang are "sitting in oblivion," "sitting and forgetting," and "fasting of the heart-mind." Chuang Tzu offers profound instructions for this practice:

> You must center your heart-mind in perfect harmony.
> Do not listen just with your ears but with your heart-mind. Do not just listen with your heart-mind but with your spirit (shen). Hearing stops with the ears, thoughts and ideas stop with the heart-mind. Your spirit, though, resides in stillness and is open and receptive to all things. True knowledge, or Tao, resides in stillness and emptiness—to attain this emptiness one must use the fasting of the heart-mind.[2]

Zuowang is a form of concentrated meditation in which the practitioner is said to achieve "the mind within the mind." We do this through seeing and listening with our spirit, our shen. The insights that arise from this kind of practice are manifold. We free ourselves from the hooks of the world and embark on "free and easy wandering" throughout the cosmos.

People new to stillness practice often have two problems: (1) too much thinking and (2) feeling sluggish or even falling asleep. If you want to get benefit from your meditation, you need to address these problems. Meditate when your energy is relaxed but not too sleepy. If you begin to feel sleepy during meditation, you can open your eyes more or rub your palms together and then rub your face. Practice a moving meditation, such as tai chi or chi gong, before you meditate. This will give your energy a way to slow down without becoming sleepy.

During zuowang practice, we are able to "forget" ourselves as a finite being and instead connect with ourselves as an infinite being, with our "authentic self." Our internal self emerges into the light of the external world. Then, by carrying that experience and perspective into our daily lives, we become free from the entanglements of dualistic mind that tend to run our world. Instead, we live our lives in a state that Chuang Tzu calls "free and easy wandering."

THE PRACTICE   Sitting and Forgetting

- As you have in other steps, put your mind's intent down into your lower dantian. This is a good way to quiet the mind, getting your focus out of your head and into your belly. By paying attention to your breath moving in and out of your lower abdomen, expanding with each inhale and contracting with each exhale, you give your mind something to do instead of running wildly with too many thoughts and thoughts about those thoughts. Counting your breaths up to nine or thirty-six, but not more than that, can also focus the mind.

- Pay close attention to your posture during meditation. You need to sit up straight, either on the edge of a chair or on your cushion. The more you slump, the harder it is for the chi to travel through your body. Your head should be pulled back a little so that your skull rests on top of your neck. The tip of your tongue should be on the roof of your mouth.

- Close your eyes halfway or all the way, as it is said that the eyes are the opening to the heart and to the shen. When you disengage your eyes from the outer world, it is much easier to use inner vision to bring internal illumination to your being.

- Sit in silence and quiescence, not thinking too much, yet not trying to force yourself not to think. Sit with a spirit of lightness and groundedness, with joy in your heart and peace in your mind.

- Sit with inner and outer relaxation—not trying to accomplish anything, just relaxing into the present moment.

- Do this for at least twenty minutes, following your breath as it enters and leaves your body. Let your spirit (shen) become light, and let your belly (dantian) become soft and open.

- When you are finished, rub your hands together thirty-six times and then slowly up and down your face.

- Do not enter the world of action right away. You will be very open and sensitive for a while, so it is best not to immediately engage with the outer world. Be gentle with yourself, be open with yourself, be at peace with yourself.

The insights and inner experience you receive with this kind of practice will change over time. Don't be in a hurry and don't be disappointed if you don't get a lot of "special effects" from your practice. Just practice diligently and regularly, and you will begin to experience the fruits of your practice. Remember, you have all the time you need.

---

1. Eduard Erkes, *Ho-Shang-Kung's Commentary on Lao-Tse* (Zurich: Artibus Asiae Publishers, 1950), 37.
2. Solala Towler, *Chuang Tzu: The Inner Chapters* (London: Watkins Publishing, 2010), 74.

17

The highest teacher is not known by others.

The next highest has followers who love and praise her.

The next highest has followers who fear her.

The lowest has followers who scorn her.

If one does not trust

she will be considered untrustworthy.

The highest teacher acts in a leisurely manner.

She chooses her words carefully

and does not waste them.

When she accomplishes things

her followers think they have accomplished it themselves.

The Commentary

There is an old Taoist tradition of being invisible to the world. This is part of being humble and not calling attention to oneself. Lao Tzu says that the highest-level teachers use their own example—how they live and how they respond to the challenges of life—in such a graceful manner that people cannot even tell they are teaching.

Many religious groups control followers through fear. People become fearful of being punished—going to hell, being reborn into a lower-level incarnation, experiencing bad karma or bad luck. They only live virtuous lives in order to escape punishment and suffering. This is not true spiritual liberation.

The highest-level teachers act in a leisurely (wu wei) manner, choose their words carefully, and don't spend a lot of time talking. When they accomplish things, they artfully arrange circumstances so students think they have done it themselves, or so that things seem to have occurred spontaneously.

Any one of us can become a teacher. We don't need special training or a certificate from a body of higher learning to influence and teach others. We, too, can be a good influence just by the way we live: responding to challenges, keeping to our self-cultivation practices, being patient and loving.

In the same spirit, everyone we meet or with whom we come into contact can be a teacher to us. There is so much to learn on this journey of ours. There are so many opportunities to grow, experience, and expand, to learn something new or be reminded of something we learned long ago but may have forgotten. We all need reminders, we all need to practice the things we are learning, and we all can always learn more. Our journey is filled with teachers, but we need to be open and greet them when they arrive. If we are filled with ego, judgment, and fear, we will never be empty enough to receive teachings.

THE PRACTICE   Letting Go

This inner journey gives us endless opportunities to learn, grow, and experience ourselves in new and deeper ways. Step 16 introduced this careful and thorough "forgetting" through zuowang practice. What are we forgetting? We are forgetting our dualistic and inflated ego, fears that hold us back, judgments that make us impatient with others, disappointments that keep us from trying again, and criticisms toward ourselves that harm or weaken our chi or lifeforce.

Another way to view letting go is releasing. What we are doing with this practice is releasing all the thoughts, ideas, and opinions about what we think we need. We practice releasing as a way to soften our heart and open our mind. In this way we will reach a state of complete openness and relaxation, which will, in turn, allow the wisdom and grace of the ancient masters into our heart-mind.

- Sit quietly and without movement, other than the slow expanding and contracting of your lower abdomen as you breathe slowly and deeply through your nose.

- Release all worries, concerns, fears, excitements, plans, and daydreaming.

- Release your need to attain some kind of higher plane of existence.

- Release your idea of what a spiritual person is.

- Release your need for approval from the higher realms.

- Release your wishes to become enlightened or attain Tao.

- Release your need to be right.

- Release your wish to become wise.

- Release your ideas about what a sage is.

- This is the practice: sitting and releasing; sitting in silent, attentive relaxation; forgetting whatever needs to be forgotten. This is the goal and the journey. This is the lesson and the reward, the challenge and the sweet spot of surrender. Spend as much time as you can in this place.

- Then, forgetting what is of no importance, recall what *is* important. Pay attention to your teachers, whether you know them or not, whether they have been in your life for many years or only showed up for a moment.

- Give thanks for all you have and all you will have. Give thanks for the challenges as well as the blessings. Remember: *with gratitude comes grace.*

18

When great Tao is abandoned
then *benevolence* (*ren*)
and *righteousness* (yi) appear.
Then intellect and cleverness rules
and great hypocrisy arises.
When the family is no longer in harmony
filial piety and duty arise.
When the country is in confusion
trouble arises.
Then come the loyal ministers.

The Commentary

When knowledge of the great Tao is abandoned or lost, it is replaced with qualities like *benevolence* and *righteousness.* These terms are used a lot by Confucius, a contemporary of Lao Tzu. The Confucians were very concerned that everyone knew their place in society and kept themselves there. The term *yi,* meaning "proper social etiquette" or "proper behavior," is used a lot in Confucian teachings. Confucius was also a big believer in the study of rituals and books. But Lao Tzu says that the highest form of knowledge is not found in these things.

Lao Tzu also takes on the Confucian concepts of filial piety and duty, saying that it is only when the family is no longer in natural harmony that striving to meet these ideals becomes important. In the same way, when the country itself loses its natural harmony, the country becomes overrun by crooked politicians—so-called loyal ministers.

Chuang Tzu says, "Our lives as well as our minds are limited. To try to understand that which is unlimited with the limited is foolish and dangerous."[1] This step encourages us to experience our unlimited self directly.

THE PRACTICE   Experiencing the Unlimited Self

How can we use our innate and natural intelligence, instead of our acquired intellect, to guide our lives? How can we fly high like dragons instead of being Earth-bound cattle? How can we go beyond "intellect and cleverness"? Taoist practices such as meditation and chi gong can help with this. They can teach us to inhabit our bodies and energy fields in grounded, solid ways. Studying Lao Tzu and Chuang Tzu helps us begin to use our mind in new ways.

Here are some sayings to contemplate. Read each one several times until it starts to take hold in your mind. Simply allow your thoughts to digest the sayings, breaking them down naturally, without any forcing or directing.

- You cannot truly grasp the unlimited with what is limited.

- Abandon hope of understanding the totality of Tao with your mind.

- Contemplate how you experience unlimited being when you open yourself to the infinite and ever-transforming Tao, through meditation, movement practice, and study.

- Contemplate letting go of your "story" and allowing ways of approaching your life from a new angle, a new process, a new way of being.

- Contemplate how, when you open yourself to new knowledge, new experience, and new ideas, you create a solid foundation that you can infinitely build upon.

- Look at your life with new eyes, from a different angle, open to receiving knowledge and wisdom from the ancient masters of Tao.

- Imagine yourself on your journey, seeing sights and wonders that you may not understand.

- Let go of trying to understand your experience with the limited intellectual mind, and feel what it's like to soar as a dragon through billowing clouds.

---

1. Solala Towler, *Chuang Tzu: The Inner Chapters* (London: Watkins Publishing, 2010), 60.

19

Abandon sageliness,
renounce intellectual knowledge,
and people will be a hundred times better off.
Abandon "benevolence,"
reject "righteousness,"
and people will naturally
return to filial piety and compassion.
Give up cleverness and discard selfishness
and there will be no bandits and thieves.
Yet these three things are considered
outward things only.
They are not sufficient.
Take this advice:
know the plain and embrace simplicity
reduce your sense of self
and lessen your desires.
Give up intellectual learning
and you will have no worries.

The Commentary

Lao Tzu advises us to abandon our illusion that we know something
about what it is to become, or be, a sage. A lot of people talk about
enlightenment, but very few really know what it means. Taoists use
the word *xianren* to describe it, which means "immortal" or "transcendent." But very few people agree on just what that term means.
Chuang Tzu offers some insight through a description of this kind
of person:

In the far off mountains of Ku there lives a holy woman whose skin is as white as snow, and who is as gentle as a child. She does not eat of the five grains but lives off air and dew. She flies through the air on a chariot made of clouds, drawn by dragons, and wanders where she pleases all along the four seas. Her spirit is so concentrated that she has amazing powers of healing and can help people bring in a bountiful harvest. She roams far and wide throughout the world of the ten thousand beings and brings them all into unity as one. She is beyond strife and confusion of the world and has no need to interact with it.[1]

Reading such a seemingly fantastical description makes us wonder how we can ever attain such a high level of being. But the reality is, we don't have to—in fact, we need to abandon the goal. All we need do is follow the last three precepts that Lao Tzu outlines later in this step.

First, he tells us to abandon acquired wisdom, or the knowledge gleaned secondhand from books. This thread runs all the way through the *Tao Te Ching*. Ho Shang Kung elaborates on this vital point when he says, "Throw away wisdom and sagacity and return to nonaction. Look at simplicity and hold fast to naturalness."[2]

Lao Tzu is a big believer in teaching and leading by example, an influence through which people *naturally* overcome the deceit of cleverness and selfishness to become compassionate. They are so inspired that there can be no bandits and thieves among them.

The inner precepts, or conditions, that will achieve this are to know the plain and embrace simplicity (pu), reduce our sense of self (thus becoming less selfish and less self-important), and lessen our desires (even our desire to be a sage or for immortality). Step 37 offers more on the concept of pu, or embracing simplicity.

None of these things can be learned secondhand; instead, they need to be experienced within our very being. Book or head knowledge is very different from heart or belly knowledge, or true wisdom.

By giving up intellectual learning and instead seeking true wisdom though the proper application of wu wei, we will learn what is truly useful. It is only in opening our minds to understanding the profound and simple knowledge of Tao that we will attain something close to immortality.

THE PRACTICE Head Knowledge Versus Belly Knowledge

There is a deeper kind of wisdom than head knowledge. This deeper kind of knowledge is called "belly knowledge" because it is not understood with your mind—instead it is understood with your dantian. When you live from your dantian, your experience is vastly different than living from your mind. You can rely on the energetic connection with the dantian that you established and expanded in preceding steps. Doing this may seem strange at first, but with practice, time, and effortless effort, it will become as natural as breathing. In this practice, you first set the intention to explore and experiment.

Whenever you read the wise words of Lao Tzu, do not attempt to grasp them with your mind; instead, let them float down into your lower dantian. Feel them pre-verbally, instinctually, in your gut. It is important to get our of your head and into your belly. Only then will much of what both Lao Tzu and Chuang Tzu are talking about here make sense for your life. Perhaps by doing this you will get a different sense of the meaning of the words.

This journey to wholeness, to a deeper understanding of yourself and your place in Tao, is filled with unexpected areas, experiences, and lessons. Because it is filled with surprises, you must keep an open heart-mind. Just remember to embrace the simple and the natural, lessen your sense of self-importance, and reduce your desire for reward. Then you will be able, as Chung Tzu says, to "roam far and wide throughout the world of the ten thousand beings and bring them all into unity as one."[3]

1. Solala Towler, *Chuang Tzu: The Inner Chapters* (London: Watkins Publishing, 2010), 9.

2. Eduard Erkes, *Ho-Shang-Kung's Commentary on Lao-Tse* (Zurich: Artibus Asiae Publishers, 1950), 41.

3. Towler, *Chuang Tzu: The Inner Chapters,* 9.

20

Give up intellectual learning
and you will have no worries.
Agreement and disagreement,
are they really so different?
Good and evil,
are they really so far apart?
What others fear, must I also fear?
This nonsense is unending!
Other people are happy
as if they are at a great feast.
In spring they merrily ascend the hills
to see the sights.
I alone remain tranquil and unmoved
like an infant who doesn't know how to laugh.
I am exhausted with no home to return to.
Other people have much
while I possess nothing.
I seem like a fool.
Other people are clear
while I alone am confused.
Other people are clever
while I seem dull.
I feel lost at sea
tossed about on the winds of a storm.
Everyone else has things to do
while I appear thickheaded and stupid.
Yet I am different from the others
because I am nourished by the Great Mother.

The Commentary

Step 20 is a big step. It is here that we leave the world of book knowledge and the left brain behind. It is now that we begin to take our first steps into the world of experiential Tao. It is here that we are marked, like Lao Tzu, as "different from the others." Hua-Ching Ni says:

> Before a human being enters the physical plane to become individualized, he or she resides in the cosmic womb of nature. In some respects this is analogous to the experience of being a fetus in the womb of one's physical mother. While contained in your mother's womb, you were one with her; whatever your mother experienced, you also experienced. In the process of birth you become separated from your mother. Your direct communication to her was cut. Similarly, before being born into this plane, we were one with nature and thus with universal law. After being born into the physical plane, we must rediscover universal law and restore our innate spiritual ability. By so doing, we reestablish our direct connection with nature, the cosmic mother of the universe. [1]

This means that Lao Tzu feeds from the source of all life, while the others, those people of the world, feed on illusions. He is connected to the beginningless and endless primordial yin, while they exhaust their yang, chasing after phantoms, all the while thinking that they are accumulating the good and important things in life.

Students of Taoism are also different from each other. They are expected to have their own ideas and approaches. While there are many paths to Tao, at the end, they all lead to the same place—immersion and connection to the divine Source of all, Tao. Many journeyers on the path to Tao would love to join a Taoist organization or travel to a Taoist retreat center, but these organizations are scarce, because most people who are drawn to this path are highly individuated, nonjoiner types who are nearly impossible to organize.

It has always been this way. Taoists are a bunch of free-thinking, free-acting, individuated individuals. They are artists, poets, musicians, hermits, healers, and diviners. In China, Taoists often travel from temple to temple, from teacher to teacher, from mountain to mountain; they are called "cloud wanderers."

Even within the Taoist temples, different people pursue different studies. One person may be drawn to martial arts or tai chi or chi gong, while others practice very deep-level meditation. Some spend hours of each day studying ancient texts, while others become healers. Of course, people are also needed to cook and clean and administer the temple itself.

As we travel on this journey to oneness, we must be prepared to deal with others, in what the Taoists call "the world of dust," who may not understand what we are doing and where we are going. Those others may even think we are deluded and going nowhere. The important thing is to remain humble and stay on the path, even if it is a pathless path. The journey of Tao is not for the dilettante or for someone who is shopping around in the spiritual supermarket. We must send our roots very deep before we can begin to spread them wide. The Chinese say that, when looking for water, it is better to dig one hole very deep than many holes in a shallow way. This journey we are on must be traveled step by step, even if one step may be much bigger than another.

THE PRACTICE Great Mother Meditation

This meditation can help connect us to the Great Mother.

- Sit or lie down and begin your deep, slow dantian breathing. Don't try to make anything happen. Don't try to feel anything special. Don't try to see anything special.

- Feel your navel, just above your lower dantian, as being connected in a very real and energetic way to the Great Mother of us all. Feel an energetic umbilical cord connecting you with your Source.

- Allow yourself to begin feeling a flow of energy between you and your original mother, what Hua-Ching Ni calls "the cosmic womb of nature." Sense this: What this mother feels and experiences, you also feel and experience.

- Draw deep sustenance from this connection. As you experience this state of being a baby in the womb of the Great Mother, feel how well you are fed by her. Draw on her strength and fill yourself with her power.

- Know that you are always connected to her, whether or not you are aware of it. Know that, as a child of the Great Mother, you are always and forever supported and loved.

- Feel how her wisdom guides and protects you. Don't be afraid to be different from the crowd. Don't be afraid to appear as a fool to others for not racing after the things the rest of the world races after. Don't be afraid to feel lost and tossed about on the winds from time to time.

- You can always remind yourself to reconnect to the Mother at any time. She is always there for you.

- When you feel you are finished, close the meditation as usual, rubbing your hands together thirty-six times and then rubbing them over your face.

You can return to this meditation whenever you feel the need to connect to the Great Mother. But also remember that you are always with her, the Source of all being, Tao.

---

1. Hua-Ching Ni, *Tao: The Subtle Universal Law and the Integral Way of Life* (Santa Monica, CA: Tao of Wellness, 1979), 31.

21

The greatest power follows from Tao.

Tao seems vague and elusive,

vague and elusive yet there is form,

vague and elusive yet there is substance,

obscure and dark yet there is essence.

This essence is real,

within it is truth.

From ancient times until now

its name does not change.

We use it to observe the origin of all beings.

How do we know the origin of all beings is this?

Through inner knowing.

The Commentary

While Tao is vague and elusive, obscure and dark, it also has substance and form. Not only that, there is a basic lifeforce contained in Tao, which we can access through our self-cultivation practice. Ho Shang Kung describes the person of Te, or spiritual power, like this: "Men of great Te are able to endure anything. They are able to take up dirt and dust and to live in humble loneliness."[1] To be a person of Te is to be a sage. Because he follows Tao in all things, he becomes filled with the lifeforce (jing) of Tao. It has always been this way. How do we know this to be true? By inner knowing.

There is a power that comes from Tao. This power can come to anyone who follows the path. It is a spiritual power that confers all sorts of things, such as inner knowing or intuition, a sense of being connected with Source, the ability to make decisions in a simple and clear manner, and the ability to live in a natural (pu) manner.

When we experience our deep connection with the unlimited, the world of the limited loosens its hold on us. In Step 18, Chuang Tzu warned us against trying to understand that which is unlimited with what is limited (our minds); however, we can *experience* it in our inner being. Then it is not just some kind of intellectual principle or idea; rather, our experience of the unlimited is something we can use to live in a whole, organic way.

THE PRACTICE   Inner Knowing

How can we experience this inner knowing? Through stillness practice, through energetic practices, and by applying the wisdom of the ancient masters to every part of our life. As Lao Tzu says over and over again, if we look at Tao and Taoist cultivation practices with intellectual understanding, we will get nowhere. Instead, we need to begin to apply to our whole life the things we learn and the things we see and experience in our practice.

The practice for this step is to choose any one of the practices from previous steps and take it further. Experience it more deeply. Pay attention while doing it in a new way, with the intention of bringing it into your entire life.

Through this deepening, you will learn how to make decisions from a place of deep knowing. Your emotions will come into balance, and you will not be a prisoner of ever-shifting emotional states. Your thinking will become clearer as your heart-mind also comes into balance. You will be able to make decisions about every facet of your life from this place of deep knowing.

---

1. Eduard Erkes, *Ho-Shang-Kung's Commentary on Lao-Tse* (Zurich: Artibus Asiae Publishers, 1950), 46.

22

Yield and become whole.

Bend and become straight.

Empty yourself and become filled.

Grow old yet become renewed.

Have little yet gain much.

Possess much yet become confused.

The sage embraces the one

and becomes a model

for all under Heaven.

She is not aggressive

and so she is able to achieve greatness.

She does not boast

and so she is recognized by all.

She does not contend with anyone

and so no one under Heaven contends with her.

The ancients said, "Yield and become whole."

Is this an empty saying?

Become whole and you will be restored to Tao.

The Commentary

The first six lines of this step are very strange to conventional thinking. Yield and overcome? Bend and become straight? How can we possibly do both these opposites? How can we *be* both? But by following the ways and teachings of Tao, it is true and possible—we learn how to be flexible yet strong, humble yet accomplished, grow older yet appear younger, have few possessions yet be happy with what we have. Only the belly knowledge or inner knowing we have cultivated in previous steps will show us how to resolve this dilemma and overcome these paradoxes.

When we get stuck, it means we are still intellectualizing and have more practice to do. We must instead feel our way into the meaning.

The sage "embraces the One," which is Tao, and becomes an example for others who may be caught up in the so-called real world. By not boasting, by being humble, and by not contending with others, we find that we have all the support we need from the spiritual world.

By taking the yin, or yielding, position in life, we become whole—restored to the Source of all, Tao. The key line in this step comes toward the end: "Yield and become whole." It is by aligning ourselves with the principle of great yin (*tai yin*) that we are able to tap into the great stream that enlivens all of life. Yielding does not mean giving up, nor does it mean giving in. It does not mean quitting. Lao Tzu is telling us to open up, to allow the flow of chi in the universe to course through our body and our mind. It means yielding all aspects of our personality and lifestyle that hold us back from connecting with cosmic flow. We give up long-held opinions and judgments about others and ourselves, letting go to still our mind.

Here is a practice that can help with this. It's a powerful way to connect with both the Earth chi and the Heavenly chi, and it can act as a tune-up for the whole body.

THE PRACTICE Standing like a Tree

This practice strengthens the kidney energy in the lower back. It will also energize the whole body, if we don't overdo it.

At first, it will be difficult to hold this pose for long, but over time, you will be able to hold it for a long time. Start with three minutes and build up to twenty minutes, if possible. If your legs start to shake, this means your legs, or chi system, are not strong. But keep going for a few moments longer before stopping. You may also experience various twitches or shaking in other parts of your body. This usually means your chi system is adjusting itself. You can either control these involuntary movements or let them play themselves out, if you are comfortable with that. Your chi body, just like your muscles and tendons, needs to adjust to changes—and this practice allows that to happen.

- Stand with your feet as wide apart as your shoulders. If you have back or knee pain, you can do this practice sitting on the edge of a chair.

- Send your roots deep into the Earth so that you are standing like a tree on the Earth, open to the sky.

- Bend your knees slightly while tucking in your pelvis, as if sitting on a high stool.

- Raise your arms in front of you, to the level of your lower dantian, as if embracing a tree.

- Your fingers should be pointing toward each other.

- Your elbows should be lifted just a little, as if you are holding an egg in each armpit.

- Feel your bai hui, at the top of your head, being pulled up slightly, as if you are being suspended by a golden thread.

- Relax your shoulders. Breathe slowly and deeply with your lower dantian.

- Place the tip of your tongue onto the roof of your mouth and smile slightly.

- Relax your whole being and extend your awareness to the world around you. Use soft focus while looking straight ahead.

- Draw healing yin chi from the Earth below you into your lower dantian.

- Draw Heavenly, starry yang chi in through your bai hui and into your lower dantian. Feel this rich yin and yang chi blending together in your lower abdomen. Picture it flowing together like in a yin/yang (taiji) symbol. Stay with this feeling for as long as you intend to do this practice.

- To end the practice, bring your arms slowly down to your sides and straighten your legs. You can shake your arms and legs out a little as well.

When doing this practice, allow yourself to really open up and receive healing energy, guidance, and wisdom from the Earth, the sky, and the stars.

To talk little is natural.

Fierce winds do not last the whole morning.

A sudden rain does not last the whole day.

Who causes this?

It is Heaven and Earth.

Yet even Heaven and Earth

cannot make such things last forever

much less can our creations last forever.

Those who follow Tao

are one with Tao.

Those who follow virtue (Te)

are one with virtue.

This person, when experiencing loss

becomes one with loss.

Those who are at one with Tao—

Tao extends toward them.

Those who are at one with virtue—

virtue extends toward them.

Those who are at one with loss—

loss extends itself to them.

The one who is lacking in trust

will not be trusted.

The Commentary

Again, we receive the advice not to expend much energy through talking and to allow silence. A big storm, with strong winds, does not last all day. The source of all these natural occurrences is Heaven and Earth, the interplay of yang and yin, being active and resting. Just as even Heaven and Earth cannot make things that last forever, neither can we. Our greatest creations will one day be forgotten, if not by us then by others.

When we identify with what is lasting, we experience ourselves as one with Tao. By cultivating virtue, or Te, we experience ourselves as being one with virtue. And by not fighting loss, we will become one with loss and we will not suffer. In addition, if we identify ourselves with Tao, we will find that the spiritual world extends itself toward us. Ho Shang Kung says, "Things of the same sort turn toward each other; harmonious sounds correspond to each other. Clouds follow the dragons, winds follow the tiger. Water flows to the wet, fire approaches the dry."[1]

If we have virtue, virtue will extend itself toward us. If we are at one with loss, our loss will be less. If we are at one with Tao, Tao itself will extend itself toward us. But if we are untrusting of others, of the world, or of our experience, we ourselves are untrustworthy. If we have trust, says Lao Tzu, trust will extend itself toward us.

Trust is a big issue for many of us, often because of past experiences, past suffering, and times we trusted and were betrayed. It is hard to maintain a sense of trust after the world lets us down too many times. As with many things, this is a matter of perspective. With time, what once felt like a deep wounding, even the end of the world, becomes clearer and easily understood as something that we ourselves set up. It may seem crazy, that we would actually set ourselves up for pain and sorrow, yet pain and sorrow, if used correctly, can be a great catalyst for change, growth, and evolution—both spiritual and emotional. Once we witness this in our lives, we realize we can trust in the ever-unfolding Tao, both in our own lives and in the life of the world around us.

Because we attract more of what we exude, it is *vital* to work with emotional states. To Taoists, emotions are seen as energetic states that rise from the five major organs—the liver, heart, spleen, lungs, and kidneys—each associated with a geographical direction, a natural element, and specific positive and negative emotions. This is part of the Five Transformational Phases (wu xing) theory, also known as the Five Elements.

One way we can work to strengthen the organs is by using the Six Healing Sounds, which is a very old energy practice that uses sounds or vibrations to affect each organ system in a positive, healing way. The sounds can balance and detoxify as well as strengthen each of our organs, which has the profound effect of bringing our emotions into balance.

THE PRACTICE   Six Healing Sounds

These sounds can be made aloud or even subvocally. The vibration in the body is the most important part. Say each sound at least nine times, slowly and deeply. You can close your eyes and imagine each sound traveling into its organ; you can also put your hands over the organ.

- The first healing sound, XU, is said to calm the chi of the liver and is made by pursing the lips together and making the sound shuuuuuu. You can imagine the color green while you are saying it. This will help with a feeling of being stuck in one's emotions or life.

- HE is said to supplement the chi of the heart. This one sounds like the "he" in the word *her*. The color to envision here is red. This will calm down the fire of the heart and induce a feeling of calmness.

- HU is to build the energy of the spleen. This one is said as whoooooooo. The color to envision here is yellow. This will help with digestion and introduce a feeling of being grounded.

- SI is said to clear the chi of the lungs. It is made with a ssssssss sound. The color to envision here is white. This will help with issues of grief and sadness.

- CHUI is said to reinforce the chi of the kidneys. It is said as chuuuueeeee. The color to envision here is black or deep blue. This will help with feelings of fear and panic.

- The last one is XI, said as shiiiiiiiii. It helps regulate the Triple Burner, which is not actually an organ; rather it has to do with the balance of the entire system.

Go slowly through each sound, and really feel each one vibrating its associated organ and inducing a feeling of deep well-being in each part of your body.

---

1. Eduard Erkes, *Ho-Shang-Kung's Commentary on Lao-Tse* (Zurich: Artibus Asiae Publishers, 1950), 51.

24

Those who stand on tiptoe
cannot balance themselves.
Those who take too long a stride
cannot walk far.
Those who show off
are not enlightened.
Those who are too aggressive
will not accomplish anything great.
Those who boast too much
will not endure.
Those who follow Tao call these things
overconsumption and useless activity.
The followers of Tao avoid them.

The Commentary

If we allow ourselves to fall into the traps described in this step, we will never accomplish anything enduring. In trying to stand out from the crowd by standing on tiptoe, we will be off balance. In trying to get ahead of others by walking fast or with too long a stride, we will exhaust ourselves. By bragging about accomplishments, especially in our spiritual life, we are indeed far from sageliness. This is like eating too much, drinking too much, grasping too much. These behaviors waste our chi and spiritual potential. Followers of Tao view such ways of being with disdain and learn to avoid them.

It is helpful to examine our life and see where we are caught up in useless activity, such as watching television, surfing on phones and computers, or engaging in mindless emotional cycles. These activities, and the people associated with them, may be draining our energy.

As we practice self-cultivation, we may find that we no longer share the same outlook on life as some of the people in our lives. We may need to drop a few friendships and reassess dynamics within our family. When someone impedes our practice, we need to step away gently and compassionately. We need all of our focus and determination to successfully complete this journey. We may even become a different person along the way.

THE PRACTICE   Inner Releasing

Letting go lightens our energetic load and allows us to become lighter in our own being. This, in turn, allows smoother and deeper communication with our higher spiritual nature.

- In a journal, list the activities, people, or even foods that impede your progress. Write about all the ways they hold you back. By first observing this, it will be easier to let them go.

- Letting go of the negativity in your life will give you much more "room to breathe." In fact, you can use the out breath to practice letting go. Hold in mind an item on your list and slowly exhale through your nose. Feel past patterns of negativity or stuck energy leave your body with your breath, emerging from your body like black smoke.

- When it is time to act, be gentle and minimize drama as you walk this path of inner cultivation and inner strength.

25

There was something formed in chaos (*hun dun*),

coming before Heaven and Earth,

existing in the silent and tranquil void.

It stands alone and unchanging.

It pervades everywhere

without becoming exhausted.

It is the mother of Heaven and Earth.

I do not know its name

and so call it "Tao."

For want of a better word

I call it "great."

Being great it is far-reaching.

It is far-reaching

yet it returns to its Source.

Therefore I say that Tao is great,

Heaven is great,

Earth is great,

and humankind is great.

In the universe, there are four greats

and humankind is one of them.

People follow the way of Earth

Earth follows the way of Heaven

Heaven follows the way of Tao

Tao follows its own natural way (*tzu ran*).

The Commentary

Chaos, what the Chinese call *hun dun,* is the original state before the formation of the world. It is a state of nothingness, or nonbeing, yet it contains the seeds of beingness. After listing its qualities, Lao Tzu admits to being unsure what to call this presence. He uses the term *Tao* almost as if pulling it out of a hat full of options. This Tao is great, as in vast and grand. Yet even though it is so far-reaching, it also returns to Source. This process of returning is Tao in the manifesting world.

Tzu ran is an important concept in the *Tao Te Ching;* it means "spontaneous," "natural," "of itself so." It describes how Taoists view the creating and sustaining powers of Tao. Tao is not a personified god-figure or creator; instead, the universe and everything in it come into being of their own accord and sustain themselves the same way. Tzu ran describes a world that is self-created and self-regulated; no creator, only the creation.

To be tzu ran is to be natural in the highest sense. If we follow the natural patterns of life, Lao Tzu says, we become a sage. The natural way is for humans to follow the ways of the Earth. We are part of this Earth, so we need to cleave to it by following the seasons of the Earth, as they manifest within as our own seasons of life.

Earth follows the ways of Heaven—the stars, the sun, the moon. The light of the sun and the tidal pull of the moon affect all life on Earth. The term "all under Heaven" (*tian xia*) includes all life on Earth. Heaven, as vast as it is, follows the ways of Tao. Tao is what regulates and supports Heaven.

As for Tao, it follows itself. Thus, the sage—or one who identifies with Tao—transcends time and place. Chuang Tzu describes this person in this way:

> The sage floats alongside the sun and moon and embraces the universe, joining it all together into one great whole. She rejects distinctions and ignores social rank. Ordinary men and women struggle and toil while the sage seems stupid and blockheaded. To her, ten-thousand years is but one. To her, the ten-thousand beings are all one, forming a whole.[1]

This road is made by walking it. This path is simultaneously carved and followed; therefore we have work ahead of us. Our journey is an opportunity, a challenge, a blessing, and a way for us to become deeper, stronger, wiser, more self-aware people. There is no one else like us in the world; there will never be anyone just like us again.

This present moment is the point of power: On this journey, we receive love and support from the spiritual realm. Each time we fall down, we pick ourselves back up, brush ourselves off, and continue. Have faith, have hope, and have patience. Travel lightly. Let go of encumbrances—emotional or physical. Float freely with the sun and the moon and the stars and embrace the universe. As Ho Shang Kung says, "To be empty is to be hollow and formless. To be unchanging is to keep the eternal during the changes."[2]

THE PRACTICE The Path of the Sage

Contemplate each of the following qualities of a sage. Let the instruction embedded in these sayings expand into your life—first in your mind's eye and then in your activity. As you do, feel your commitment to becoming a sage strengthen.

- Sages reject distinctions and ignore social rank.

- People of tzu ran don't care how society sees them.

- They do not need the approval of society to know they are on the right path.

- They honor their teachers and respect their students.

- They take care of their body and uplift their spirit.

- They balance their energy and live a life of gratitude and grace.

- They look within to their innate wisdom and to the ancient wisdom of the great teachers of Tao.

- They are fully engaged with the world, yet are not overly affected by it.

- They feel a deep and grounded connection to the Earth and are also connected with all under Heaven.

- Their life is not run by their emotions.

- They are not proud; they are humble.

- They are not aggressive; they embrace the yin.

- They do not overextend themselves in an effort to appear youthful to others; they age gracefully and are eternally youthful in spirit.

- They do not demand love from others; they give love freely.

- They float along with the sun and the moon and embrace the whole universe.

Can you be like this, expressing the attributes of a sage? Can you be humble enough and loving enough and open enough to receive the wisdom of the ancient masters and make it your own? What's stopping you?

---

1. Solala Towler, *Chuang Tzu: The Inner Chapters* (London: Watkins Publishing, 2010), 39.
2. Eduard Erkes, *Ho-Shang-Kung's Commentary on Lao-Tse* (Zurich: 1950, Artibus Asiae Publishers, 1950), 52.

26

Heavy is the root of light.

Tranquility is the master of agitation.

Therefore the sage travels

without leaving sight of his origin.

Although there are beautiful things to admire

he is indifferent to them.

He is like a lord of the thousand chariots

yet he takes himself lightly.

To act too hastily is to lose one's root.

Hasty action will make us lose our self-mastery.

The Commentary

Ho Shang Kung says, "The blossoms and leaves of the herbs and trees are light, therefore they are perishable. The root is heavy, therefore it is lasting."[1] And when Lao Tzu speaks of tranquility as the master of agitation, he is pointing to the power of Taoist meditation, or stillness practices, as the base for movement practice. Out of deep stillness, movement is created. Transformation is then possible, as Ho Shang Kung amusingly says, "The dragon is quiet, therefore he is able to transform."[2]

As spiritual journeyers, we too must travel far without losing our connection to our own Source. There will be many attractions and distractions along the way, but we must not let ourselves be drawn off course by them. We can experience ourselves in a noble way, as "lord of a thousand chariots," yet we cannot take ourselves too seriously. By moving in a hasty or ungrounded manner, we will lose our way.

All of this is possible because we are so strongly rooted in Source, like a tree growing from the Earth. When we imagine a tree, we picture a trunk with limbs, branches, leaves, and flowers or fruit. Yet underground is a part of the tree that is as big as, or even bigger than, the growth we can see. Only with strong, "solid" root structure can trees resist being knocked down by winds. And so it is with us: when our roots are strong and stable, we are able to take ourselves as lightly as a bird resting on a thin branch. We can have many responsibilities, like the lord of a thousand chariots, yet step lightly on the Earth and in our own dance of life.

THE PRACTICE   Rooting and Grounding Practice

Heavy, says Lao Tzu, is the root or foundation of light. We need to have a solid foundation if we want to spread our wings and fly. If we have nothing to push off from, we will gain no momentum. By sending roots down deep and breathing up the good, yin energy of the Earth, we can ground and stabilize in any moment. This practice is useful to do before tai chi or chi gong practice. It can also be done any time we feel tense or even frightened.

- Stand or sit on the edge of a chair, with feet planted firmly on the ground or floor. Close your eyes, breathing deeply and slowly through your nose. Place the tip of your tongue on the roof of your mouth. Spend a few moments doing this.

- Then, with your mind's intent, send roots into the Earth from the bottom of your feet, from a point called *yong chuen,* or "bubbling well point," in the ball of your foot. Send these roots down at least three to five times the length of your body. See the roots extend deep into the Earth, past all the dirt, stones, animal burrows, and any roots from plants in the area. Really dig down deep into the Earth.

- Feel yourself become very strong and very stable, like a tree. Feel yourself ready to bend with the wind, yet remain standing.

- You can also send any stress, pain, disease, or discomfort down through those roots so the Earth can soak it up.

- Draw up good yin sustenance from the Earth, as your roots dig down to reach, absorb, and send this nourishment up to your branches and leaves. Feel the Earth's nourishment rise through the bottom of your feet, then up your legs, hips, shoulders, down your arms, and into your head until your whole body is filled with the good rich yin energy of the Earth.

- Stand or sit in this way for a time, feeling yourself as a tree with roots burrowing deep into the Earth. Your head or bai hui is open to receiving the Heavenly energy from above, while your roots dig deep into the Earth.

- In this way you become a vital and strong being, open to receiving healing chi from above and below.

- When your practice time is over, draw your focus back up into your physical body, while still experiencing yourself as deeply rooted. Stay with this feeling the rest of the day. In this way, all of your actions and movements will come from a rooted place. You may notice that your walking changes, as well as the ways you move and interact in the world.

---

1. Eduard Erkes, *Ho-Shang-Kung's Commentary on Lao-Tse* (Zurich: Artibus Asiae Publishers, 1950), 54.
2. Ibid., 55.

Those who are good at walking leave no tracks;

those who are good at speaking make no mistakes;

those who are good at calculating need no counters;

those who are good at closing things need no lock

yet what they close cannot be opened.

Those who are good at tying

use no rope,

yet what they tie cannot be untied.

This is why the sage is good at helping people

and abandons no one.

She is good at caring for things

and so rejects nothing.

This is called *penetrating brightness*.

Therefore the good person is the teacher

of those who are not so good.

Those who are not so good

are the students of the good person.

If one does not honor one's teacher

and if the teacher does not love her students,

although there will be much knowledge,

there will also be much confusion.

This is called *great mystery* (*yao miao*).

The Commentary

For those on the Way, the path does not come with street signs or way posts. Our own footprints, as we travel, are so light, we do not leave tracks. Because we are careful with our words, we lessen occurrences of mistakes and miscommunication.

The sage is always open to others and never rejects or judges what comes her way. This is called penetrating, or perpetuating, brightness. The written character for "brightness" is ming, which is a picture of a sun and a moon side by side. It stands for clarity of vision and understanding. In sages, this has such brightness that Lao Tzu calls it "penetrating brightness," indicating mystical vision and deep understanding.

"Great mystery," or *yao miao*, describes something that is passed on, or transmitted, from teacher to student. It works in a mysterious way because it is done without words. This is considered the highest form of teaching in Taoism.

On this journey, we will encounter teachers all along the way. At times it will seem that everyone we meet is in some way a teacher. We must also remember to share with others whatever wisdom or guidance we receive from these teachers. We cannot judge who is worthy of such guidance, but must give it freely—as we ourselves received it. Chuang Tzu says:

> If we follow our true nature, who will be without a
> teacher? Must it be that only the ones who understand
> the cycles of change have a teacher? Without knowing
> this deep mind and insisting you know what is right and
> what is wrong is like leaving on a journey to Yuen today
> after having arrived there long ago.[1]

Once, while having dinner with my friend and Taoist teacher Hu Xuezhi up in Wudang Mountains, one member of my tour group asked him about nei dan, or inner alchemy. His advice was simple: to really study inner alchemy seriously, he said, "You need to become a farmer."

In this case, he was not giving career advice but was telling us we would need to live a very simple life, with little distractions. We would need to have no family, he told us, and thereby no responsibilities for anyone else so that we could apply ourselves totally to our own cultivation practices.

Yet we *can* live "in the world" and do deep cultivation practices. It is not necessary to drop out and go live in the mountains or "become a farmer" in order to do spiritual practices. It is by living with an attitude of gratitude and grace and openness to learning from all our teachers, physical as well as nonphysical, that we can make our way on this great pathway to Tao.

THE PRACTICE The Path of Refinement

This is a path of endless refinement: refining our energy, chi, spirit, and understanding. As we become more refined, lessons do not need to be as harsh as they were at the beginning of the journey, because we are more open to learning and changing. We are more sensitive, which can bring the blessings of appreciation and acceptance. This sensitivity can cause discomfort as well, because old habits no longer insulate us. Many lifestyle choices that we used to make no longer work for us, and while this can feel uncomfortable and even painful at first, it is crucial to choose new ways of living if we are going to become more refined in mind, body, and spirit.

As you become more sensitive, pay attention to what you are choosing in all aspects of your life. Here are some examples of how choice might affect you during the journey. Contemplate how these, and other, refinements are occurring in your life. This is inner alchemy, in which your coarse nature becomes more refined over time to become something else entirely, like transmuting lead into gold.

- Foods that you used to eat with no problem suddenly become a problem.

- Friends that you used to enjoy now seem too coarse and are not pleasant to be around. It is possible to become so sensitive that it can be difficult to live in today's environment. Even in ancient times, practitioners moved to the mountains or countryside, where life was slower and less complicated. You may experience this desire to simplify your environment. You can also have a simple and refined life even in the midst of a big city. It is up to you to use your cultivation practices to create a grounded and simple lifestyle, wherever you are.

• While you may not be able or willing to drop your possessions, family, and career to go into the countryside and become a farmer or hermit, you can extricate yourself from fragmented society.

• You do not have to spend your days glued to a smartphone, computer, or television.

• You can spend more time in nature, which may mean the great nature outside of yourself or the great nature inside of yourself.

• You can pay attention and be alert for lessons when you meet a teacher, whether one who teaches by good example or one who teaches through bad example.

• You can consciously allow your energy and spirit and life to become more refined.

---

1. Eduard Erkes, *Ho-Shang-Kung's Commentary on Lao-Tse* (Zurich: Artibus Asiae Publishers, 1950), 54.

28

Know the strength of the masculine

yet preserve the feminine.

Remaining receptive to all under Heaven

do not separate yourself from the eternal virtue (Te).

Become again as a child.

Know the white (yang)

but embrace the black (yin).

Serve as a model for all under Heaven.

Serving as a model for all under Heaven

and not deviating from the eternal virtue

one returns to the primordial origin (wuji).

Know honor yet maintain humility.

Be as a valley for the world.

Being as a valley for the world

remain in touch with the eternal virtue.

Return to the simple and natural (pu).

When the wood is carved

it becomes useful

yet the sage remains with the simple and natural.

Thus her carving injures no one.

The Commentary

Know and honor the strength of yang, the masculine nature of Tao, but embrace the strength of yin, the feminine nature of Tao. This tells us to keep our receptive nature open to all under Heaven while, at the same time, remaining connected to primal virtue. How can we do this? To be "in the world but not of it"? We don't run away or shut ourselves up in a high tower of spirituality while looking down upon the world with disdain. We don't only honor our "higher" divine self and denigrate our "lower" animal nature. We embrace both aspects to live in the world in a balanced way. Taoists are fully engaged with the world, reveling in the wondrous creation that surrounds us, the "ten thousand beings."

As part of the same instruction to find balance, Lao Tzu invokes yang and yin through the colors white and black. Ho Shang Kung says, "Whiteness exemplifies enlightenment, blackness silence. Though a man may know himself as enlightened and penetrating, he must keep this state by being silent, as if he were in the darkness and invisible."[1] By doing this, we attain wuji, which is the vast emptiness that gives birth to all form (taiji). The symbol for wuji, the source of all, is an empty circle.

Lao Tzu recommends returning to the simple and natural, the uncarved block, or pu. Pu is a simple, uncluttered, and natural way of being in the world. We return to being the block of wood in its natural state, before the woodcarver—or society—has taken a chisel to us. Sometimes we become shaped into an unnatural form due to childhood training or even abuse. To release these patterns, we need to become as the uncarved block of wood—simple and unformed. This does not make us stupid and dull; rather, we return to who we were before being rigidly chiseled by parents, schools, religion, and society.

In the same way, Taoist spiritual cultivation does not force us to become something we're not. Any chiseling we do cuts away extraneous layers of ego, pride, selfishness, "head" knowledge, and even our pain to reveal our true and natural state. This takes practice, much practice, but if we truly wish to return to Source, to the wuji, we need to flow through life like water so that in each moment we can allow the tai chi dance to express itself through us.

The theme of this step is to know and maintain the strength of yang while at the same time preserving the strength of yin. Harmony is all-important, as too much of only one side leads to disharmony, which manifests as problems, stress, and disease. This includes harmony of yin and yang, inward and expansive energy, quiescence and activity, internal and external, nonbeing and being. All need to be in balance, though this does not mean each side is exactly equal at all times.

Sometimes we are up, sometimes we are down. Sometimes our energy needs to move out, sometimes we need to pull it in. Sometimes we are fully engaged with projects like writing, playing music, cooking, and traveling, and other times we are in retreat, preferring to reflect and absorb through reading or listening deeply to ourselves and the world. The balance point is thus found by knowing when to be in yang mode and when to be in yin mode.

THE PRACTICE Learning Your Balance Point

The practice of tai chi is not done at only one time and in one way. Rather it is to be aware of the shifts in our being at all times, so that we know when to act in a yang fashion and when to act in a yin one. Here is a good way to feel the moving balance in ourselves, internally as well as externally. It is drawn from tai chi practice.

- Begin by doing the rooting practice from Step 26. Be sure to send your roots down into the Earth at least three to five times the length of your body.

- Allow your breath to slow down until you are breathing slowly and deeply from your lower dantian.

- Put your weight on your left leg and lift your right leg slightly (more if you can). Your left leg is your yin leg, rooted deep in the stillness of the Earth.

- Allow the right leg to be light and buoyant, ready to move as inspired or directed. This is now your yang leg, full of activity.

- Take a step forward with your yang leg. Pour your weight into it; feel it become heavy and still as it now carries your body.

- Feel your left leg, which was previously filled with yin, become light and eager to move.

- Then take a step forward with your left leg, placing it on the ground, your weight shifting so your right leg becomes light and buoyant.

- Alternate back and forth from one leg to another for a few moments, feeling your weight shift back and forth.

- You can take slow steps forward or backward or move in a circle. You can even begin to dance, feeling the transition from yin to yang in your body as various parts and limbs carry the spectrum of energies, balancing themselves as you move.

- To conclude this practice, spend a moment reviewing where in your life you are overextending and where you are pulling back. Think about how you can find a more stable, balanced center point in your life.

---

1. Eduard Erkes, *Ho-Shang-Kung's Commentary on Lao-Tse* (Zurich: Artibus Asiae Publishers, 1950), 58.

29

Those who desire to control Heaven and Earth

will not succeed.

The world is sacred.

One cannot grasp it or control it.

Those who attempt to control it

will ruin it.

Those who attempt to grasp it will lose it.

It is natural that

sometimes it is right to move forward

and at other times to follow from behind.

Sometimes breathing is easy

and sometimes it is difficult.

Sometimes we are strong

and other times we are weak.

Sometimes we are up,

sometimes we are down.

Thus the sage avoids extremes and excess

and rejects extravagance.

The Commentary

This step offers guidance on nonstriving and our tendency to think we can control the world. The world is sacred, says Lao Tzu, and as such, whoever attempts to control it is doomed to fail. In our modern world, despoiling nature in an attempt to control it has led to climate change and the possibility of ending both animal and human life on our beloved Earth.

Just as Taoists venerate the cycles of nature, we honor the changes in ourselves. Sometimes we are up, and sometimes we are down.

Sometimes we lead from out front, and other times we lead from behind. Sometimes our life is easy, and other times it is hard. Sometimes we are strong, and other times we are weak. The practice of flourishing and maintaining a peaceful center in the midst of all this rising and falling is to avoid extremes, excess, and extravagance. We don't become too excited about the ups, nor too depressed about the downs. By taking a middle path between extremes, the sage is able to live his life in simplicity and peace of mind.

THE PRACTICE   Useful Versus Mindless Activity

Ho Shang Kung says, "Spiritual things like peace and rest. They cannot be governed by activity."[1] Too much activity, especially mindless activity, drains our chi and disturbs our shen.

- In a journal, reflect on what activities you are involved in that contribute to this loss and disturbance, such as watching too much television, bad eating habits, obsessive thinking, or engaging in toxic relationships.

- Record your activities in your journal for a few days. Then see which ones contribute to your journey and which do not. Ask yourself: Which activities should I drop, and which ones do I need to keep?

- This practice is also about finding a balance between too much activity and too little. Too little activity will cause problems with stuck, slow-moving, or stagnant chi. Too much activity will result in loss of chi.

- Experiment with holding to your center and letting your inner knowing tell you the right direction for this day or this moment. Remember that your point of balance is shifting all the time. What may be the right decision one day will be wrong another day. Do not hold on to any one way or direction. Know that Tao is always shifting and moving, and your place on the wheel of existence also turns each day, bringing you to a new place in each moment.

---

1. Eduard Erkes, *Ho-Shang-Kung's Commentary on Lao-Tse* (Zurich: Artibus Asiae Publishers, 1950), 59.

30

Those who use Tao to assist the ruler

do not use military force.

This kind of force has a way of backfiring.

After a great battle comes years of famine.

A skillful ruler achieves his purpose

without using force.

Achieve success without being aggressive.

Achieve success without being arrogant.

Achieve success without thought of gain.

Achieve success without using force.

Too much force will result in loss of strength.

Even the strong eventually grow old and weak.

This is called *going against Tao.*

Anything that goes against Tao

will come to an early end.

The Commentary

After a battle, the land is ruined, crops are destroyed, and the people suffer. This is an image used to describe the outcome of a ruler who seeks to create an empire by war. It can also describe the person who seeks to conquer the world by attempting to force life to conform to their wishes. The people around them end up suffering. And their use of force backfires. The outcome is they suffer.

Skillful people do not use force to get what they want out of life. To achieve success in life, we must not be aggressive, arrogant, or attached to the outcome of our efforts. We avoid attempting to force things to happen the way we want them to, which is another teaching on the way of wu wei. By using too much force, we end up losing strength or missing our goal. Even the strongest people experience old age and weakness. The use of force goes against the flow of Tao—and nothing that goes against the flow of Tao lasts.

We all want to be successful in life. Unfortunately, many people will do almost anything to achieve that success. They will step on others, cause pain and suffering for profit, accumulate the negative karma of wishing harm on enemies, and even destroy their own health. Success means different things to different people—some want material wealth or fame, others want to make a living doing what they love to do, regardless of pay.

However, forcing or going against nature (especially your own true nature) will be short-lived and possibly even harmful. Lao Tzu describes a different way; a way in which it is possible to achieve success without using force, being aggressive or arrogant, or even thinking of our own gain. Chuang Tzu says:

> It is easy to cover one's tracks, but to walk without touching the ground, this is difficult. You have heard of flying with wings, but it is indeed difficult to fly without them. You have heard of the knowing that comes from the result of knowledge, but you do not yet know the knowing that comes from not knowing.[1]

To reach our goals in a balanced and harmonious way, doing no harm to others or oneself, to be able to walk without touching the ground and fly without wings, is difficult. Yet to walk on without knowing just where this journey will take you, to be able to use "not knowing" as your guide—this is true cultivation!

THE PRACTICE   Journaling Your Journey

This step offers the opportunity for us to decide just what we want to achieve in the short time we have and to contemplate how we want to do it.

- Journal in depth about what success means to you. What does it feel important for you to achieve in this life?

- Ask yourself: How can I accomplish that without harming myself or others? How can I do it while nurturing my health, family, and friends?

- Now, contemplate how you can apply the teachings of Tao to achieve success—materially or spiritually—using the least amount of effort.

- In your journal, write down the steps you feel you need to take to do this. Know that if you are truly humble in your journey, there will be teachers and guides present all along the way.

- Contemplate how your journey is as important as your goal, if not more important. Ask yourself: How can I take these steps along my journey and stay close to Tao, acting in ways that will bring long-lasting results and greater peace of heart-mind?

- As you step forward, write in your journal regularly or whenever you feel moved to do so. When you feel stuck, as if making no progress, look back in your journal to see that you have indeed traveled far.

- Make your journey one step at a time—sometimes with baby steps, sometimes with bounding leaps.

---

1. Solala Towler, *Chuang Tzu: The Inner Chapters* (London: Watkins Publishing, 2010), 76.

Weapons are inauspicious things;
all living beings hate them.
Those who align themselves with Tao
turn away from them.
The follower of Tao
gives favor to the left (yin) side.
The followers of war
give favor to the right (yang) side.
Weapons are inauspicious things
and the wise person only uses them
when there is no other way.
They do not see beauty in weapons.
They do not exalt in killing.
Those who exalt in killing
will never achieve themselves.
Victories in battle
should not be celebrated with joy.
Instead they should be celebrated with sorrow.
This is why a great victory
should be followed by funeral rites.

The Commentary

The *Tao Te Ching* was written in a time of war, a time in Chinese history known as the Warring States Period. Lao Tzu, who worked in the capital of Zhao, was sickened by this and decided to leave his high position to strike out for the wilderness. Perhaps he felt that the wilderness, as dangerous as it could be, was not as dangerous as the human wilderness of warriors and political strategists that surrounded him. Weapons, he says, are inauspicious, and all living things are repelled by them. Ho Shang Kung elaborates on why: "Weapons excite the spirit and dim the harmonious atmosphere. They are evil tools. One ought not to use them even if they are ornamented."[1]

The person of Tao views weapons as inauspicious and only uses them when there is no other way. He does not see weapons as objects of beauty, no matter if decorated with fine jewels and etchings, because they have a way of turning on the wielder. He does not exalt in killing. Those who do will never achieve great things in life—they may have great power over others, but inside they are lost.

Weapons have many different forms, as does the harm they cause. They can be sharp and metallic, or they can be verbal, emotional, energetic, or psychological. Sometimes we aren't even aware we are using such weapons on the ones we love or on ourselves. Victories in battle should not be celebrated in joy, Lao Tzu tells us, but marked by the sorrow that many have died. Victory should include honoring those who have given their lives on both sides, as whatever we gain in a victory, we gain because someone else loses.

The followers of Tao, Lao Tzu tells us, favor the left, or yin, direction, while the followers of war favor the right, or yang, direction. In the *I Ching* (*Yi Jing*) we find the left direction associated with the element wood, symbolizing new growth, spring, and the blooming of new life. The right direction is associated with the element metal, symbolizing the season of autumn, when the cycle of blooming is over, the cycle of withering begins, and the cycle of dying is near. Of course, metal is also associated with weapons.

THE PRACTICE Not Wielding Weapons

This guidance on the use of weapons, in whatever form they take, offers us an opportunity to reflect on our relationship to weapons. In your journal, reflect on and answer the following questions:

- Do you own any weapons?

- If you do, are they objects of beauty? Self-defense? Are they for sport or for another purpose? How do they contribute to your life? How do they detract from your well-being or the well-being of other humans and living creatures? How do you feel when you use them? In what other ways do you arm yourself?

- If you do not, how do you feel when you look at a weapon? Do you feel fear, loathing, or judgment? In what circumstances might you use a weapon? And if you are without training in using any weapons, do you feel defenseless or strong? How do you arm yourself instead?

- How do you arm yourself verbally? Do you try to defeat people with insults?

- How do you arm yourself intellectually? Do you try to defeat people by destroying their logic? Do you use mental games to outwit and weaken opponents? Are you capable of bending the truth just to win an argument?

- How do you arm yourself emotionally? Do you have outbursts that wear down your opponent? Do you withdraw into a cold silence to draw out the weaknesses of the other person?

- How do you arm yourself energetically? Are people immediately drawn to you or repelled by you? Once you let them get close to you, do they turn away? Do people receive what you have to say, or does something in your delivery keep you from affecting listeners?

- Look at all the weapons you have discovered that you wield. Which among them can you do without? Might there be ways of feeling safe, of experiencing beauty, of getting what you want that rely on other tools and skills than wielding weapons? Contemplate any intentions that arise as a result of this practice.

---

1. Eduard Erkes, *Ho-Shang-Kung's Commentary on Lao-Tse* (Zurich: Artibus Asiae Publishers, 1950), 62.

Tao is eternal and nameless.

Though it seems simple and small

no one under Heaven can control it.

If princes and kings

could rule in accordance with it

all beings would naturally obey them.

Heaven and Earth would be

mutually joined in harmony,

causing sweet dew to fall upon all.

The people, without being ordered,

would come into harmony naturally.

It is when we begin naming things

and thinking we have control of them

that we need to know when to stop.

Those who know when to stop

avoid coming to harm.

Tao in the world

is like a river flowing into the sea.

The Commentary

Tao may seem very simple and natural and perhaps easy to control, yet it cannot be controlled. If the rulers would take on some attributes of Tao—such as pu (humility or being natural)—then people would instinctually follow them. Their entire kingdom would come into harmony on its own, and everyone would benefit.

By naming things, we think we gain control over them. To name something is to mistakenly think we have knowledge about the world and the way it works. The more we think we have power, the less we actually have. It is when we think we have gained the upper hand in our lives that something happens to remind us that control is impossible.

In our journey, we have to stop attempting to control everything and instead admit to not knowing. In this way, we will prevent harm. Lao Tzu reminds us to practice the Watercourse Way if we want to live with peace and tranquility. Life becomes a river flowing ever onward, to the sea.

THE PRACTICE   Life Review Practice

Naming things and thinking we have power over them can lead to headaches and disappointment. Surrendering to each and every moment, to the greater good and the greater whole, to Tao, will help us recognize and experience true power. This step offers the opportunity to reflect on where we struggle with control. Here are some questions to consider:

- Do you struggle to control what you eat and don't eat?

- In what ways do you attempt to control the people in your life?

- How do you try to control people and outcomes at work?

- Are you trying to force progress in your spiritual journey?

- How would it feel to release each of the ways you attempt to control?

- Would an open-minded and open-hearted approach change anything, internally or externally? How?

By following the Watercourse Way, we can release control and flow with the currents and whirlpools of our life in healthy and fulfilling ways. Movement practices, like tai chi and chi gong, help us experience the Watercourse Way in our physical and energetic body. The slow and graceful movements introduce us to flow and balance. This is how, in ways that cannot be understood intellectually, we can align with the flow of nature and Tao.

If you have not yet established a regular movement practice, this is a good time to do so.

33

To know others is wisdom

but to know one's self is enlightenment.

Those who conquer others

require great power.

But to conquer one's self

requires inner strength.

Those who know they have enough

are already wealthy.

Those who persevere have strong will.

Those who are not separated

from their center will long endure.

They can die but will not perish.

They will become an immortal.

The Commentary

This is one of the most important steps on our journey. It is not enough to understand the ways of others; what we really need to know and understand is ourselves. We can become wise in the ways of the world, but to attain Tao, we must know ourselves deep down into the darkness of our being. Then, in bringing that darkness to the light, we become enlightened—full of light. Lao Tzu uses the word *ming,* as he did in Step 27. Ming is a light that shines beyond what we can see with our eyes. We can only see this ming by looking with the inner eye.

While we can overpower others, to have real power, we need inner strength. This is a different kind of strength than the one we use for control. This kind will endure: it is not flashy but steady, not forced but flowing, not pushy but yielding, not harsh but gentle. It is real power, the power of Tao. Using it takes a strong will—but not a will of iron.

Instead, it requires the soft strength that is able to bend with the wind and flow with the current. People with this kind of strength know they are wealthy if they have just enough to live. They are connected to their center, their root, their innermost being. In this way, they not only endure, but they also achieve a state of immortality.

THE PRACTICE Knowing Yourself Through Gongfu

The term *gongfu* (*goong fu*) means any skill that is learned through hard work and practice. It does not mean martial arts, which are called *wushu,* though it can mean martial arts if that is something one learns through deep practice. It can also mean gardening, cooking, painting, carpentry, tea ceremony (see Step 77, The Way of Tea)—anything that we put time and effort into learning and perfecting. It is about going deeply and applying ourselves wholeheartedly to any skill or project, including cultivating our connection to Source, or Tao.

Knowing others is easy, says Lao Tzu, knowing yourself is hard. It takes dedication and hard work, yet it is the most valuable goal of all. The best way to accomplish self-knowing is through gongfu practice. The inner attentiveness and self-cultivation of gongfu can be applied to any activity. You can practice it more formally in tai chi or chi gong movement forms, tea ceremony, or calligraphy practice. You can also practice it in all your activities: while engaging conversation, cleaning house, gardening, driving in traffic, responding to emails, or painting a landscape. Do what you love with the idea of gongfu. To attain self-knowing through gongfu is to attain true power.

Remember, gongfu means something that takes practice to master. There is a reason these meditations and movements are called *practices.* You are practicing something, over and over, in all the various ways your life presents itself to you, in order to get good enough to be called a master (*shifu*).

Taoist practices are lifelong practices; they come from the *yang sheng* (*nourishing life*) tradition. Therefore, they are not something you do for a little while and then master. Instead, view them as the central axis around which your life spins. When you practice self-cultivation in a gongfu fashion regularly, you are in touch with Source and live close to Tao. Apply yourself wholeheartedly and let the spirit of gongfu uplift your being. Then your practice will become the beautiful dance that you are.

34

Great Tao flows everywhere
both left and right.
All beings depend on it to live.
It holds nothing back.
It accomplishes much
yet makes no claim to it.
It nourishes the ten thousand beings
yet does not act as their master.
We can call it small
yet all beings return to it
and it does not act as their master.
It can be called great
yet it does not strive to be great.
In this way it achieves greatness.

The Commentary

Tao is primal chi that nourishes all living things. It is in the smallest forms of life and yet it contains all that is. It is great in the sense of noble, grand, and universal, but it does not strive to be great. It does not strive to be anything other than what it is, and it is therefore truly great. Once again, Lao Tzu assigns words to the nameless, images to something beyond form, and meaning to a state that transcends all.

What do we identify with? Do we identify with our small and limited sense of self or with our ever renewing and inexhaustible Source? Of course, it is much easier to identify with our small self, as that is what presents itself to us on a daily basis. It is much more difficult to identify with the great Tao.

THE PRACTICE The Wordless Journey

As in Step 33, it takes practice, diligence, and openness of spirit to experience ourselves as one with Tao.

- Think of something like a beautiful sunset or a lovely flower and try to describe it to someone else without using words.

- What kind of gestures or facial expressions can you use to express the image?

- Now, think of something a little more subtle, like an emotion or idea or concept you want to share with someone, again without using words.

- How can you share an idea or concept or vision with others without relying on words, or left-brain activities?

This exercise teaches us a lot about how we rely on words or mental or intellectual ways of communication when there are so many other ways to communicate. As Lao Tzu tells us in the very first step, Tao cannot be described in words but only experienced directly. Our journey is made up of each step we take, each breath we take, each small bit of understanding we reach, each instant of time we spend in the timeless zone, each moment of letting go and letting be, each time we are able to spend identifying with our "higher self," our true source.

The one who holds to the great image of Tao—

all beings under Heaven will follow him.

They will come to no harm,

only peace and contentment.

There is fine food and music

and travelers come by and stop.

Yet to speak the word Tao

is tasteless and has no flavor.

If one tries to see it, it cannot be seen.

If one listens for it, it cannot be heard.

Yet it will never be exhausted.

The Commentary

In another beautiful description of the follower of the Way, Lao Tzu shows how, by holding fast to the reality of Tao, a sage draws people to her. They come to no harm. With fine food and lovely music, travelers are drawn by feelings of safety and peace (*tai ping*). A person of real power has an aura that attracts. People feel drawn to her, sometimes without knowing why. People feel lighter, as if cares and woes have lessened. This person exudes joy and wellness, laughing often and deeply. The atmosphere feels as if a feast is happening, with music playing lightly. A sage like this serves as an example for what is possible to achieve through self-cultivation. Even though Tao is elusive, the sage shows us it *can* be approached, union with Tao *can* be achieved, and we *can* become greater than we are now, deeper than we are now, wiser than we are now.

Without taste and no flavor, Tao is invisible and silent. How can something so elusive have so much power? In the world of dualism, we view power as something tangible, obvious, and "real." It's expressed through brute force or clawing to the top. Powerful people are the ones in charge—the boss, the king, or the queen—the ones with all the money, fame, and knowledge.

It is futile to merely speak the word *Tao* and think that is the experience of Tao. The actual experience of Tao goes beyond mere words and naming. When we try to see Tao with our limited vision, we cannot see it. When we try to listen to Tao with our limited hearing, we cannot hear it. Yet this same Tao is never exhausted and ever renewed. This is why the one who has true power is the humble one, the quiet one, the one who no one notices, the one who yields before might, who bows to the unknown, who appears dull and stupid, who, like in Step 20, bends with the wind and flows like water.

THE PRACTICE   Becoming Who You Really Are

In your journal, reflect on and answer the following questions:

- How can you become who you really are, your true unlimited self?

- What is stopping you from achieving this level of being?

- How can you let go of your worries and fear?

- How can you put aside any petty dualistic mind frames and enter into this deep relationship with Tao?

One way to do all this is to stay true to your journey and to the directions and instructions you receive along the way. And, most important, it is in actually *applying* these instructions and lessons to your daily life. Enlightenment, illumination, immortality—all are reached one step at a time. You cannot end your journey before you even begin. Even the "sudden illumination" school of Buddhism and Taoism recognize that what may appear "sudden" is the result of many small steps along the way.

As with the stone steps in the mountains of China—some of which are tall and some short, some wide and some narrow, some newly built and others crumbling and potentially dangerous—each of your steps will be different from the others and will present different challenges. Yet if you stay with this journey and do not quit too easily or lose your way in gaudy attractions along the way, you will arrive at the end a different person, someone of whom it can be said, "all beings under Heaven follow her."

36

If you want to restrain something
you must first expand it.
If you wish to weaken something
you must first strengthen it.
If you wish to abandon something
you must first elevate it.
If you wish to acquire something
you must first give it.
This is called *subtle illumination* (*wei ming*).
The soft and weak
conquer the hard and strong.
Fish cannot leave the water.
The great weapons of a nation
should not be shown to anyone.

The Commentary

This verse might not seem to make sense at first. How does expanding something help contract it? How does strengthening something make it weak? And how can giving something help us acquire it? It is very difficult to understand because we have been raised to believe that up is very different from down, that large is very different from small, that high is the opposite of low, and that strong is the opposite of weak.

Lao Tzu is showing us the cyclical nature of all things. When we work within these cycles, we can dance with them gracefully, rather than fighting harshly. One way leads to health and spiritual evolution, and the other leads to frustration and disease. To live within these cycles is called *subtle illumination* (wei ming). We become very subtle and operate in ways that are hidden to most. Yet throughout our lives, we all go through cycles. Even within one day, these cycles can move powerfully, because we, like the universe itself, are governed by natural laws. These are natural laws of give and take, going and returning, losing and receiving. To understand and apply these laws in a conscious way adds a subtle, yet powerful, illumination to our lives. What appears strong today may appear weak tomorrow. What appears right today may appear wrong tomorrow. The follower of Tao knows this and does not grasp one part of the cycle while refusing the next part.

As Lao Tzu says, fish cannot live outside water—when they are taken out, they suffocate and die. In the same way, we live in Tao while striving to take ourselves out of oneness and into the world of duality. We are like fish, slowly suffocating ourselves by straying from our true nature; with roots in the formless, we suffocate in the world of form. To return to the world of Tao is to return to the water that we came from, the water that nurtures us.

One of the most important lessons in this step is that in order to receive, we must first give—especially when we don't think we have anything to give. Once we have emptied ourselves of all that we think we know and are, we will find the hidden gem of our own Tao nature, deep within the cloud of our unknowing. This is also the key to weakness overcoming strength.

Subtle illumination is another key to understanding Taoist cultivation practices. They are not showy and do not attract attention, because those who cultivate Tao "speak softly and act with care." They are as careful at the beginning of a journey as at the end. They rest in the knowledge that what has lasting value is not the most glittery jewel but the humble stone, the same stone that has the power to wear away at egotistical and dualistic mind-sets—which most of the world revels in.

THE PRACTICE The Soft Overcoming the Hard

The idea that the soft can overcome the hard challenges a society where "might makes right" and where the strong can always beat the weak. The practice for this step encourages us to start contemplating how the soft overcomes the hard, how we teach without words and do by not doing. We are engaging the following questions:

- How can what is soft and weak overcome the hard and strong?

- How can we strengthen something by first weakening it and weaken something by strengthening it?

- How can we get something by giving it?

In your journal, identify the areas of your life where you feel strong and where you feel weak. Have you always felt that way, or have things changed over time? Was it you that changed or the circumstances? If you think of each situation in terms of cycles, has anything come back around? If you can identify where you are in the cycle, can you see what is coming next?

Once you have done that, think of something you want. Can you apply what you are sensing about cycles so that the empty place you feel now can be filled with what you want? Is there something in the way that you need to let go of first? Think of how you might give that thing away, to someone who will appreciate it, to the universe, or even returning it to the Earth. Then, think of how you can ask for what you want. Is there something you can give away that symbolizes what you long to receive? Or that, in the act of giving, invokes an experience? Again, you can give it to a person or to the universe and your helping spirits. But the most important question is: What can you give?

Take some time to think about these things. It is good to know what you are asking for, what you are willing to work for, and what you are willing to give up in return. Meditate, ask for guidance, breathe deeply. Only when you are empty of grasping will you attain anything.

37

Tao does not act

yet there is nothing that it does not achieve.

If people could uphold this

then everything would transform itself naturally.

If they still desire to act

they should themselves return

to nameless simplicity (pu).

By returning to nameless simplicity

there is no desire

and with no desire

things return to tranquility.

Then all under Heaven

will naturally calm themselves.

The Commentary

Tao is the ultimate example of wu wei. Tao does not act, as a human acts, as deities of various religions act—yet in that nonaction, there is nothing that Tao does not achieve. Nature does not leave out any steps in its process. Everything is done in its natural time, and everything is complete in itself. If we can apply this level of harmonious nonaction to our own lives, our personal cultivation would also develop in a natural fashion. If we find ourselves trying to act or to force something to happen, then it is best to simply return to the formless. With meditation and nei dan practice, we arrive back in a state where our lives unfold naturally and simply.

When we regard the world as static, with humans as the only active agents, then we carry the burden of responsibility for the world. This creates superiority and the right to dominate. But if we see ourselves as merely one part of the whole—one aspect of a vast, transforming collection of all living beings—we will understand and experience ourselves as true spiritual beings.

As spiritual beings, we transform in each moment. Most people do not notice: they think they have been the same forever and will be the same until they die. While externally changing diet, hair color, and musical taste, inside they think they are static. But in truth, we are in a constant state of self-transformation (*tzu hua*). Hua-Ching Ni says,

> All physical beings are transforming. No one stops
> transforming for even a single second. With or without
> your knowledge, the transformation process constantly
> and subtly keeps going on.[1]

This is the second time Lao Tzu uses this word *pu,* which means "simple," "unadorned," "something in its original state." The Japanese have a wonderful aesthetic that captures the spirit of pu, called *wabi sabi,* which is an appreciation for things in their natural, imperfect, worn state. Examples include crafting lumpy, odd-shaped *raku* pottery; using raw bamboo utensils for tea ceremony; or building a sacred tea hut from recycled materials. People can be wabi sabi, too. A perfectly natural person, with all her lumpy edges and imperfections, is closer to the truth of how a spiritually developed sage is than any ideas about a pristine, perfect saint. The difference between a sage and the average, spiritually sound-asleep person is that a sage is aware of her imperfections and is able to use them creatively and openly. She is therefore able to be perfect in her imperfection, simple in her inner being, and natural in her dealings with the world.

THE PRACTICE Change, Transformation, and the Art of Imperfection

When faced with a great challenge in life—an accident, health scare, or near-death experience—we often change significantly. We are shaken so deeply that we have no choice but to change who we are in very real and fundamental ways. But wouldn't it be nice if we could affect those kinds of positive changes without almost dying to do it? Wouldn't life be fascinating if we could allow ourselves to be the transformative beings we rightfully are? Wouldn't it be wonderful to find a way to dance with change rather than fight it? What's stopping us?

- Take the time to reflect on, or write in your journal about, your resistance to change and transformation. Do you view yourself as a static being who has been in a fixed state since the day you were born? Pick a past event that marked a milestone in your life. Are you the same person now as you were then? If you were to experience the same thing again, would things feel different?

- Now, consider how you might be holding onto an ideal self. Is this self an epitome of perfection, making no mistakes and expressing with flawless control? Probably not.

- Take a step toward your imperfections by listing them in your journal. They can be physical, emotional, or behavioral; they can be activities you flounder at or talents that have been undeveloped.

- Read through your list and apply the wabi sabi aesthetic of appreciating the faults, finding beauty in the accidental or broken, and celebrating the richness in the imperfection. See if you can approach the perfection in your imperfections.

- The last practice in this step is to return to contemplating change and transformation. Does it seem so scary now?

---

1. Hua-Ching Ni, *The Gentle Path of Spiritual Progress* (Santa Monica, CA: SevenStar Publications, 1987), 366.

step

38

Superior virtue (Te) is not superficial,

this is why it is superior virtue.

Inferior virtue is always superficial.

For this reason, it is not true virtue.

The person of superior virtue acts

without intention (wu wei).

The person of inferior virtue

acts with intention yet achieves nothing.

A person of superior benevolence (ren)

acts without intention.

A person of superior righteousness

acts with intention yet without thought.

A person of ritual acts, and there is no response.

He rolls up his sleeves and begins to force others.

When Tao is lost, what remains is virtue.

When virtue is lost, what remains is benevolence.

When benevolence is lost, what remains is righteousness (yi)

When righteousness is lost, what remains is empty ritual (li).

Those who emphasize ritual

bring about superficial words and much confusion.

Small knowledge reduces Tao to flowery phrases.

This is the beginning of foolishness.

This is why the sage dwells in the profound

and not on the superficial.

He dwells in the solid and not the flowery phrases.

He leaves *that* and sticks to *this*.

The Commentary

This step is a critique of conventional notions of spirituality. Lao Tzu opens by distinguishing between superior Te and superficial Te. What is the difference between the two? When the practitioner develops his own Te—not by actions, but by his very being—he aligns with Tao and the natural currents to support him. That is the highest level of Te. The other kind of person works very hard to achieve special powers or spiritual insight, but ends up wasting time and can only achieve a superficial, lower-grade Te.

The Chinese character for ren, or benevolence, is an image of a person and the number two. Lao Tzu is describing the process by which a person steps out of Tao and into the dualistic world of human society—immediately dropping down a level to benevolence, an unnatural state of false virtue. From here he drops down another level to righteousness, which Lao Tzu sees as an artificial form of virtue because it is handed down by the ruler to the rest of society. The next level down is "empty ritual." The problem Lao Tzu has with this is that rituals set up a space between the person doing the ritual and the original nature of Tao—thus separating them. Ritual becomes important only because humankind has fallen so far away from its original Tao nature. Ritual is not useless, but if we were still connected to our source, we would not need to be so pushy and demanding for results that, in the end, don't happen.

The sage dwells in the profound, not on the superficial. It is easy to get caught up in the superficial aspects of the world, as distracting and dazzling as they are. It is challenging to find our way to the profound and then, once we have found it, to stay with it. Many pathways veer off in many directions. Some look promising and even spectacular, but they are all distractions to our journey. How do we stay on our path? By not getting caught up in *that*—the world of form and distractions—and instead choosing *this*—the simple, natural world of Tao.

One of the tools for staying on the path of Tao is the *I Ching* (*Yijing*), also known as *The Book of Changes* or *The Book of Transformations*.

The *I Ching* is the oldest book in the world, perhaps 6,000 years old. Long known as a book of divination, the *I Ching* is also a manual for self-cultivation. It applies principles of Taoism to life circumstances, particularly wu wei. Through the *I Ching* it is possible to receive guidance and information about various forces influencing our situation at any point in time. We then create our future through how we work with, or even play with, these forces. In this way any situation, no matter how challenging, can be used to take another step along the path of self-cultivation.

THE PRACTICE The *I Ching*

To learn ways of being wu wei in any life situation, we can consult the *I Ching*. It offers alternatives to our strong urge to change situations that feel uncomfortable or painful. Typically, when we feel stuck, we want to break through to the other side. Yet, when we fight hard to change our situation, we often make things even worse. The *I Ching*'s advice is to hold fast and do nothing, conserving our chi until things change themselves. This ancient book and the guidance it contains detail how to flow *with* the changes that life offers us instead of fighting against them.

When using the *I Ching* as a divination tool, it is important to approach it with humility and an open mind. The book itself is a conduit for spirit, Tao, or our higher self to speak with us. If we open our heart-mind to receive guidance and information, we create a resonance within the universe that will be responsive. On the path of Tao, it is said that "thoughts are louder than thunder."

Many versions of the *I Ching* are available, and all offer instructions on how to use it as a source of contemplation and study, as well as a divination tool. Of course, I am partial to my teacher Hua-Ching Ni's version, published as *The Book of Changes and the Unchanging Truth*. I feel his version comes closer to using the *I Ching* as a method of self-cultivation than many of the others I have seen.

There are many ways to do a reading. Here are some basic tips for bringing the *I Ching* into your journey.

- Sit for a while and meditate on your question. The more centered and clear you are, the easier it will be for the spirit of the *I Ching* to speak to you. As Chuang Tzu says, we cannot see our clear reflection in running water, only in still water.

- If you need to make a decision about something, it is better to ask two related questions—for example, (1) What would be the outcome if I did plan A? and (2) What would be the outcome if I did plan B? Sometimes doing plan A looks very good, and you might feel tempted to go ahead with it, but then when you look at plan B, it turns out to be even better!

- It is not appropriate to ask yes/no questions of the *I Ching*. The book conveys a lot of subtlety about your situation and never offers black-and-white answers.

- The ancient wisdom of the *I Ching* can feel difficult to understand. It will become clearer as you use it and as you work on your own self-cultivations practices.

- Allow the guidance of the ancient masters to permeate your being, using your belly knowledge instead of your head knowledge.

39

In ancient times, all things

had attained the One.

Heaven attained it and became clear.

Earth attained it and became peaceful.

Spirits attained it and became active.

The valley attained it and became full.

All these things attained the One.

Thus the ten thousand beings

attained the One.

Kings and rulers achieved it

and ruled all under Heaven.

Because of this I say:

If Heaven were not clear it would shatter.

If the Earth is not peaceful it will collapse.

If the spirits are not strong they will wither away.

If the valley is not full

it might become exhausted.

If the ten thousand beings did not arise

they could be extinguished.

If rulers are not loyal to the people,

their honor will be lost and they will be toppled.

The high must take humbleness as its root

and take the low as its foundation.

This is why true princes and kings

refer to themselves as *orphans* and *worthless*.

Do they not take humbleness as their root?

Therefore high praise is really not praise.

For this reason one should not desire

to be exquisite like priceless jade

but rather humble like simple stone.

The Commentary

This verse describes the world in order, as it is, at peace in restful movement. In this step, we can simply relax and sense what this feels like. In the beginningless beginning, all things align themselves with the One (Tao). Heaven, Earth, the valley spirit, and the other countless spirits all align themselves with Tao. All living things (the ten thousand beings) align themselves with Tao. Kings and rulers, also, when aligned with Tao, are able to rule over vast kingdoms.

Yet if the very heavens are not clear, they will shatter; if the earth is not peaceful, it will collapse; if our spirit is not strong, it will wither away; if the valley spirit is not full, it will become exhausted; if all living beings do not arise and achieve themselves in Tao, they will be extinguished; and if the very rulers themselves are not loyal to the people they rule, they too will lose their place in the world.

Empty words and flowery praise are not to be trusted. The true sage does not covet things like exquisite jade but holds himself humble as a simple stone.

THE PRACTICE   Full Moon Meditation

This practice can be used when we want to explore the feeling of being One, when we need a reminder or want to relocate our center, or whenever we long for Tao. It is also helpful when we are struggling to sleep or when we just need to find a calm space within ourselves.

If you do this practice in the evening, be sure to allow the energy of the moon to move down to your lower dantian. If too much energy stays in your head, it could keep you from sleeping.

- Sit or lie down. Close your eyes and begin doing dantian breathing.

- Instead of breathing in and out of your nose, you can breathe in through your nose, or Gate of Heaven (*tianmen*), and then out through your mouth, or Door of Earth (*dihu*). Picture these two places opening and closing as you breathe in and out.

- In your mind's eye, see the bright full moon hovering just overhead.

- Feel its golden light pouring down over the top of your head (bai hui) and then through your central channel (*chong mai*) down into your lower dantian, filling it with the rich yin energy of the moon.

- You can also allow it to enter your body through your upper dantian (third eye) point.

- Feel the soothing yin energy of the moon filling your own being with peace and relaxation.

- When you are finished, rub your palms together thirty-six times and then place them over your eyes, breathing the warmth of your palms into your eyes and then back into your brain.

40

Returning is the motion of Tao.
Gentleness (*ruo*) is the function of Tao.
All things under Heaven
are born from existence.
Yet existence is born of nonexistence.

The Commentary

Returning, or reversion, is the instruction to bring our awareness from the world of duality back to the world of oneness or nonduality. This is the mystic quest in Taoism. Gentleness, or ruo, is the nature of Tao. *Ruo* can also mean "yielding," "soft," "supple," or "flexible." In Step 36, Lao Tzu introduced us to *ruo neng ke gang*, "the soft overcoming the hard." This gentleness has much strength within it.

All things under Heaven originate from nonexistence. In Steps 1, 14, and 25, Lao Tzu described how all form originates from formlessness. We, too, as part of this world, have our origin in formlessness. How powerful it is to truly understand this. Ho Shang Kung tells us:

> Heaven and Earth, the spirits, and everything flying and creeping originate from Tao. Tao is formless. Therefore they are said to originate from nonexistence. This means that the fundamental vanquishes the external, that weakness vanquishes strength, and humility self-contentedness.[1]

The mystic quest in Taoist practice is to return from the world of form back to the world of the formless. Here is an illustration of that process. It is an ancient illustration called the *Taichi Tu* (*taiji tu*), or Diagram of the Great Ultimate, and it is more than a thousand years old.

This diagram illustrates the mystic quest of Taoism, the return to oneness. The top empty circle represents wuji—the original, primordial state of being. Moving down, the next circle is yin/ yang (taiji), where the original, undifferentiated primal energy of the universe begins to transform into the two primal forces of the universe, yin and yang. The black is the quiescent force, and the white is the active force. From there, the journey moves into the Five Transformational Phases (wu xing), where yin/yang further transform into the five basic elements of life: wood, fire, earth, metal or gold, and water. This is the world in which we live, where things are in a constant state of transformation.

The small empty circle beneath wu xing is said to be the "grounding force" between the four others. Under that is an empty circle that represents the melding of the Heaven and Earth energies, which create all of life as we know it. The last circle represents the "ten thousand beings"—all life in the manifest realm.

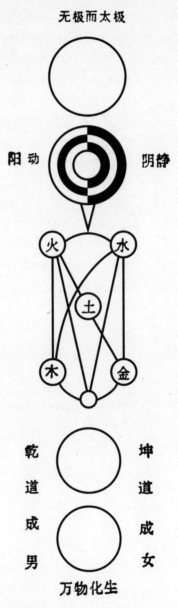

Diagram of the Great Ultimate[2]

THE PRACTICE   Returning to Source

When we use the power that the material world gives us—our chi, heart-mind, intent, and ability to focus and persevere in self-cultivation practice—we will move up from the bottom of the image, through the various circles, up through the wu xing and taiji symbols, and then back to the original, pure wuji state. This is the path of return from the world of the myriad beings to the Source of all being.

- Through the ages, people have found this diagram helpful, as it is a roadmap of our journey. Call this image to mind as you read the rest of the book. See if you can track where you are at any given point.

- Keep your eyes and mind on this road while staying open to the wonders that offer themselves to you along the way. Delight in them, while not being pulled away from the path. Take your time, keep your heart open, remember to breathe, remember to laugh. In this way, your journey will be a celebration of returning home.

---

1. Eduard Erkes, *Ho-Shang-Kung's Commentary on Lao-Tse* (Zurich: Artibus Asiae Publishers, 1950), 78.
2. Image from Hua-Ching Ni, *Mysticism: Empowering the Spirit Within* (Santa Monica, CA: SevenStar Publications, 1992), 70.

41

When the superior person

hears about Tao

she practices it diligently.

When the average person

hears of Tao

she practices it one moment

then loses it the next.

When the inferior person

hears about Tao

she laughs at it.

Yet if we do not laugh

we will never know Tao.

Therefore these things are said:

The bright Tao

sometimes seems dark and obscure.

Advancing on the path of Tao

sometimes feels like retreating.

The smoothness of the path of Tao

sometimes feels bumpy.

The superior virtue of the path of Tao

sometimes feels like an abyss.

The perfect clarity of Tao

sometimes seems spotted.

Great virtue

sometimes feels insufficient.

The most well-established virtue

appears weak.

The pure truth of Tao

sometimes appears changeable.

The great square has no corners.
The perfect tool
is sometimes completed last.
The perfect note
is sometimes hard to hear.
The perfect image is without form.
Great Tao itself
appears hidden and nameless.
Yet Tao nourishes all things
and brings them all to fruition.

The Commentary

The first part of this step compares the different levels of spiritual aspirants. They are either inspired or frustrated that the true understanding of Tao is very difficult to obtain, especially at first. The teachings, while simple, can often seem hard to understand, even obscure. And as we travel on our journey, we may feel we are taking two steps backward for every one forward. We may even feel we are losing ground. This is very common and nothing to worry about.

Our journey may feel a bit bumpy at times. We may even feel we are on the edge of a deep abyss. We may not feel clear about where we are going, our energy may feel weak, our understanding may change from day to day. This journey has no defined parameters. The most important tool or vessel is often the last one made, in an "aha!" moment. The perfect note, or taste, of wisdom is often hard to hear if our ear, or palate, is not accustomed to it.

The perfection of Tao seems to be hidden from us. Tao itself appears hidden and nameless. This is because it is the nameless, mysterious (xuan) origin of all things.

THE PRACTICE Sense of Humor Is Essential

A sense of humor is good with any spiritual path, but it is crucial with Taoism. Taoist texts, especially *Chuang Tzu,* have traditionally used humor in their teaching stories. Here's one from *Chuang Tzu.*

> Chuang Tzu and his friend Hui Tzu were crossing an ancient bridge over the Hao River. Chuang Tzu said to his friend, "These fish we see below us come out and swim about so leisurely. This is the joy of fishes."
>
> Hui Tzu turned to him and said, "How do you know what fish enjoy? You are not a fish!"
>
> "You are not me," answered Chuang Tzu, "so how would you know what I know about the joy of fish?"
>
> "Well," said his friend, indignantly. "I am not you and so do not know what you know. But, as you are certainly not a fish, there is no possible way that you can know what fish enjoy."
>
> "Ah, then," said Chuang Tzu, who was dipping his fingers to play in the water as little fishes came up to nibble them. "Let us go back to the beginning of our conversation. When you asked me 'How can you know what fish enjoy?' you knew that I knew. The reason I know this is by walking over the river!"
>
> As was the usual case in these kinds of conversations with his friend, Hui Tzu glared at Chuang Tzu, who was languidly moving his fingers in the water and chuckling to himself.[1]

Keeping a good sense of humor will help a lot on this journey. At times the road will be rough, the weather uncertain, and you may feel you are not making any progress. But keeping a sense of proportion and a sense of humor—along with a good helping of patience—will make the journey much easier.

Laughing at yourself is always good medicine. Laughing at the absurdity of life will get you very far down your path. Being overly sober about the spiritual path will actually stop your progress. So enjoy your journey, even the most challenging parts, and you will be able to travel as if on the wings of a dragon or a butterfly.

---

1. Solala Towler, *Tales from the Tao* (London: Watkins Publishing, 2010), 166.

42

Tao gives birth to the one.

The one gives birth to the two.

The two gives birth to the three.

The three gives birth to the ten thousand beings.

The ten thousand beings all carry yin

and embrace yang.

Harmony is achieved by blending these two things.

People look down upon the solitary,

the orphans, the widowed, and the unworthy

yet the nobles use these terms for themselves.

In this way, one loses by gaining

and gains by losing.

What others teach, I also teach:

those who use violence

will not die a natural death.

This is my fundamental teaching.

The Commentary

This step talks about the origins of the universe and our place within it. Tao itself, as the nameless and formless Source, gives birth to the One—which is form. This One then brings forth the two primal energies of yin and yang, or Heaven and Earth. From the interaction, or blending, of yin and yang, three is produced: Heaven, human, and Earth. From three, all living things are birthed.

All life, the ten thousand beings, turn toward the sun (yang) with their backs toward the Earth (yin). Earth, or the cosmic yin, is our origin, and the sun, or cosmic yang, is our destination. With a foundation in yin, we can soar into the yang. We need to blend both aspects if we are to proceed on our journey in a harmonious way.

On the path of Tao, while it may seem that we are giving up a lot—ingrained bad habits, false egos, attachment to the world of dualism, and any propensity for violence—in truth it is only by "losing" these things that we gain complete understanding and healing.

THE PRACTICE   Nonviolence Toward Yourself

Violence can take many forms; it can come from the outside world as well as from within us. Sometimes others inflict violence upon us, and, at other times, we lash ourselves with emotional, psychological, or even spiritual weapons.

- In your journal, make four columns each on two pages. The first page is for external violence that you have experienced, or are experiencing, in your life. Label the columns as follows: "Physical," "Emotional," "Psychological," and "Spiritual." Do the same on the second page, which is for internal violence.

- Take a moment to feel rooted in the Earth and as if you are reaching to Heaven. Feel all judgments of yourself or others leave your body.

- Allow a word or phrase that captures an experience of violence to arise. It could be names of people or places; it might be something you say to yourself or that others said to you; it can even be the age you were when an event occurred.

- Write this word, phrase, or image down on either page in the most relevant column. Write down as many things as arise in you.

• Consider how your experience of abuse from others went deep within you, so that you are now your own abuser. This is especially common with childhood abuse.

• When you feel complete, look at all the forms of violence in your life. Begin to ask yourself, How can I stop this and find a new way forward?

• You can establish a foundation for a new way forward by learning to still your madly spinning mind. Meditation, tai chi, and chi gong practices can help with this, because they help you detach from the illusions that you think are real.

• Although your experiences are real in the world of duality, once you learn to detach from a dualistic mind-set, you will see, as Chuang Tzu says in Step 45, that this is all a dream and one day you will wake up and see it for what it truly is.

43

The most yielding under Heaven

overcomes the hardest under Heaven.

What has no form can enter

where there is no space.

Because of this I know

that nonaction is most beneficial.

Teaching without words

and doing without doing—

few people understand this.

The Commentary

There is a story in the *Chuang Tzu* that describes wu wei as it is lived. A prince is told that there is a Taoist master working in his kitchen. Curious, the prince descends into the bowels of the vast kitchen and finds a cook who, though he has worked there for many years and has cut up countless oxen, has never needed to sharpen his cleaver.

When the prince asks the cook how this is so, the cook replies, "It is simple, my lord. I am a follower of the Way in everything that I do. When I began to cut up oxen, all that I could see was the part of the ox in front of me. After three years, I was able to see the entire ox in one glance. Now, I no longer use my eyes but my chi. This is how I let the knife itself follow the grain of the meat. I let the knife slice its own way through the openings of the joints and the hollows of the ox, never touching the tendons or ligaments, much less the bone. By following the natural way and letting the knife do the work on its own, I have become a master carver.

"Sometimes I come upon a difficult cut. Instead of wielding my blade harder, I stop completely and meditate upon the situation. I look very closely at the joint and move my blade very, very slowly, using no force, until suddenly, plop, the meat falls away like a clump of earth falling to the ground. Then I stop and look around me to see if I am still in accord with the Way. If I am, I am happy. Then I wipe my blade very carefully and put it away. I am finished."

"Aha," said the prince. "From hearing the words of this wonderful cook, I have learned the art of nourishing life (yang sheng)."[1]

THE PRACTICE   Road Rules

- Pay attention to "yield" signs.

- Practice being "formless."

- Don't force anything.

- Keep your eyes, or attention, on the prize: spiritual enlightenment.

- Share your space.

- Avoid "road rage," which is ineffectual striving through driving.

- Enjoy the view.

- Listen to the soundtrack of your mind, but don't get caught up in it.

- Laugh at yourself.

- Worry less; celebrate more.

- Give yourself some slack.

- Pay attention to the people in front of you and behind you.

- Watch for signs along the way.

- Look out for animals and other helpless creatures.

- Be careful not to miss your exit or entrance.

- Don't listen only with your ears but also with your heart; don't listen only with your heart but also with your whole being.

- Honor your teachers.

- Don't resist; rejoice.

- Love the whole world as if it were your own self.

---

1. Solala Towler, *Chuang Tzu: The Inner Chapters* (London: Watkins Publishing, 2010), 60.

44

Which is more desired: fame or life?

Which is greater: life or material wealth?

Which is more harmful: gain or loss?

Excessive emotions will cause great suffering.

Piling up of material wealth will cause great loss.

Those who know when they have enough

will suffer no disappointment.

Those who know when to stop

will not experience disgrace.

They will live a long life.

The Commentary

The first line of this chapter uses the word *ming* once again, only this time it means "name." Having one's name well-known is a form of brightness and fame. For some people, this is very important. Yet for the followers of Taoism, life itself is much more important.

Then we are asked what is more important to us—material wealth or life itself? Which is more harmful—gain or loss? Because gain becomes a weight in our life, the more wealth we accumulate, the more we worry about losing it. Any excessive emotion causes even more problems: psychological, emotional, and energetic.

The one who knows when he has enough does not have anything to worry about. Another way to say this is, the one who knows when he has enough will always have enough. Knowing where and when to stop accumulating prevents the suffering and disgrace that come with loss or disappointment. Preserving the chi we otherwise waste on worrying about the future frees it up for uses in our day-to-day life and spiritual self-cultivation. We feel at peace with ourselves and the world around us.

It is fine to have goals and work to achieve them. It is fine to be financially solvent; it is better to support yourself and not rely on someone else. Begging for our food is not a Taoist tradition.

THE PRACTICE Strengthening Your Spleen's Earth Energy

While life itself is much more valuable than any material wealth can be, living in poverty is a big drain on our chi. Constant worry about money damages our shen, our spirit, as well as the Earth energy that is held in our spleen. Too much worry and self-absorption lead to this deficiency; in the same way, having weak spleen energy, caused by bad dietary habits, causes us to worry more. The sign of a spleen deficiency is reviewing a problem or a concern incessantly in our mind or speech. Some of the things that weaken our spleen energy are too many grains, too much sugar, and excessive amounts of processed foods.

Here is a practice you can do to bolster your inner richness by strengthening the spleen's Earth energy.

- As described in Step 23, the sound associated with the spleen is HU, or whoooooooo. Make this sound frequently throughout your day.

- As you do, visualize the sound as a yellow light, which is the color associated with Earth energy.

- Add some movement by standing or sitting in a chair and—as you make the sound—raising your right arm up in front of you, palm down. As you reach the level of your head, turn your palm up, and raise your arm all the way up, giving yourself a good stretch.

- At the same time, lower your left arm down in front of you and stretch it toward the ground.

- Then inhale and stretch each arm the opposite way.

- Make the sound HU throughout the movements and envision your spleen becoming strong and healthy so it can do a good job of digesting the food you eat—as well as the experiences in your life.

- Do this three, six, or nine times on each side.

45

The greatest achievements seem imperfect
yet their usefulness will not grow old.
Great fullness can seem empty
but if one uses it wisely
it will not become exhausted.
The straight may seem crooked;
great skill may seem clumsy;
great speeches may seem awkward.
Activity will overcome coldness.
Calm stillness conquers heat.
Tranquil stillness balances
all things under Heaven.

The Commentary

By understanding things as Lao Tzu describes them in this step, we arrive closer to home, to our Source, to Tao. The last four lines give us very practical advice about finding balance in our life.

This step brings home the message that when we see with our outer eyes and depend on that to decipher what is "real," it can be deceiving. Only with inner vision can we see what is real and true and distinguish that from what is illusion—what Chuang Tzu calls "the dream."

Those who dream of a great feast may wake up
and weep the next morning. Those who dream of
weeping may actually enjoy a great hunt the next
day. While they are dreaming, they do not know they
are dreaming. In the middle of a dream they may
even try to interpret their dream! It is only after they

awaken that they know they had been dreaming. At
the time of Great Awakening we will all wake up and
see that it has all been just a dream.[1]

When we are dreaming, says Master Chuang, we think the dream is real
and are either happy or sad about it. Then, when we "awaken" the next
day, we realize it was a dream and stop being happy or sad about it. Yet,
that night or even the same day, we enter another dream and are happy
or sad about that. This is why almost everything we see and experience
in our so-called life is part of this dreaming. All our problems and challenges are part of the dreaming. All our attempts to break out of the
dream are also part of the dream. So how are we to know what is "real"
and what is the dream?

Waking up from the dream is a path of letting go of all self-
limiting ideas, fears, and habits. From early age, they are passed on
and ingrained within us by our parents or society. We think that these
things form the way the world works; we don't question them. Then,
we pass these same ideas, fears, and habits on to our own children. It is
a vicious cycle that never ends, unless we decide to wake up and let go
of the ideas, fears, and habits accumulated over one or many lifetimes,
unless we open ourselves to the possibility of being an awakened being
in each moment.

THE PRACTICE Tranquil Sitting

Another way to wake up from the dream is with tranquil sitting
(zuowang). When we practice tranquil sitting, we do so with a light
heart. We sit with joy, with a spirit of letting go of anything we don't
need, in order to reach a state of deep inner peace.

- Relax your face muscles into a small smile. Don't sit with
  a frown or a grimace. Think of statues or paintings of
  the Buddha and Taoist masters in meditation and recall

whether they frown or grimace. Try smiling, just a little, next time you meditate. You will be amazed by how much it lightens your spirit.

• When you meditate, don't try to stop the wild horse of your mind—but don't give in to it either.

• Meditate with the desire to wake up, to let go of bonds that hold you down and restrict your movement between worlds. This is a time to let go of bad habits, fears, laziness, or anything that is holding you back from waking up.

• Sit with fierce determination, as well as a soft joyful acceptance of yourself, exactly as you are right now.

• Sit up straight, do not slump; yet do not hold yourself too rigidly either.

• Learn to dance with the dream.

• Don't let the dream bind you, don't let it hold you back, don't let it determine who and what you will be.

• Follow the Watercourse Way and flow with the dream, all the while knowing that the dream is not real.

• In this way you will be one of those people who the ancient Taoists called "seed people" (*zhongmin*). The seed people are the ones who advise others on how to wake up. They are the ones who have already woken up, sometimes in another lifetime. They have come here in this lifetime to remind us of who we really are.

- When you enter the realm of tranquil sitting, allow the seed person you truly are to emerge.

---

1. Solala Towler, *Chuang Tzu: The Inner Chapters* (London: Watkins Publishing, 2010), 39.

46

When Tao is present in the world
horses are used in the fields.
When Tao is not present in the world
war horses are bred outside the town.
There is no greater curse
than not knowing when one has enough.
There is no greater misfortune
than the desire for material wealth.
Only those who are satisfied with what they have
will always have enough.

The Commentary

When the teachings of Tao are present and things are in harmony, horses are used to plow the fields. They are in the center of our creativity, and their strength is used for farming. But when things are not in harmony, which in its extreme is during war, the same horses are bred as warhorses. Their strength and power are located far away from the fields and homes of the townspeople.

Not feeling we have enough—money, respect, love, or anything—leads to depression, anger, and stress. Lao Tzu considers racing to accumulate more of anything, with no regard for mental, physical, or emotional health, to be a kind of curse. Racing after material goods that we think we need to make us happy is a curse that we create for ourselves. On the other hand, if we are satisfied with what we have, we are content. No matter how much or how little we have, it is enough.

THE PRACTICE The True Heart

Being content with what you have brings comfort and good psychological, emotional, and spiritual health. Ho Shang Kung calls this state "preserving one's root" and having "a heart without desires."[1] The heart that is always desiring more is called the False Heart. The heart that knows when it has enough and is content with what it has is called the True Heart.

Here are some teachings to contemplate for cultivating your True Heart.

- Think of what you have that you are content with, rather than what you do not have.

- You can lead a very simple life without rushing around after wealth and acclaim.

- This journey you are on is long and winding. The more baggage you are carrying, the harder it will feel. This is why letting go, not only of worldly possessions but also of the *desire* for them, is so important on your journey.

- This doesn't mean you need to be poor and homeless or not own anything of any value. What is more destructive is the desire for material wealth and the never-ending quest for it. That is what disturbs internal harmony. The outcome of insatiable desire is a very sad and frustrating life, as well as a level of stress that can make you sick.

- Being without desire doesn't mean you can't work for what you want in life.

- It doesn't mean you have to live a life of serious asceticism.

- Being without desire means you can be happy with what you have; if that changes and you have more, you can be happy with that.

- And if you lose some of what you have, you can be happy with that.

- In the end, after your body gives out or is damaged beyond repair, all you are left with is the love you have shared and the fruits of your spiritual cultivation. Nothing else.

---

1. Eduard Erkes, *Ho-Shang-Kung's Commentary on Lao-Tse* (Zurich: Artibus Asiae Publishers, 1950), 86.

47

Without going out your door,

you can know everything under Heaven.

Without looking out the window,

you can see the Tao of Heaven.

The farther one travels

the less one knows.

The sage knows without traveling

sees without looking

and accomplishes all without striving.

The Commentary

We are on an inner journey. We can take this journey without leaving our front door. The farther we travel from the root, or source, of life, the less we actually know. We may think that, because we have gone to universities and received degrees and such, we know a lot. We may feel that we are old enough to have experienced plenty of life and are therefore wise. But actually, most of us know very little of what is real and true and lasting.

Even inside our home, we can still travel far, see many things, and understand more. By spending time journeying within, we will see all sorts of wonders. We don't need to even look outside to see amazing things. In fact, only by looking inward will we see and experience such things. Each step within is another step toward wholeness, healing, and complete identification with Tao.

THE PRACTICE   The Inner Journey

This is a journey we can engage right where we are, at any given point. This spiritual quest is the journey we take to arrive at the root of our being, our True Heart. Here are some guidelines.

- This journey you are on is full of surprises and lessons and takes you farther than any outer journey can—even if you were to travel around the world.

- If you travel anywhere in life without seeing with inner vision and without looking deep into the window of your heart-mind, it will be as if you never left your illusion-filled house, constructed from delusion and desire.

- When you do travel in the outer world, it is possible to go everywhere and yet learn nothing about yourself at all. You may enjoy seeing the sights, eating the food, and hearing the sounds of another culture, but if these things do not teach you something about yourself, you will end your journey in the same place you started from.

- Spiritual pilgrimage, on the other hand, takes you to foreign lands in a different way: you strive to discover something new about yourself as you discover a place.

- The sage does not need to travel to foreign lands to learn about herself.

- As in Step 1, the sage sees without looking.

- She learns about herself and her relationship to Tao effortlessly, without striving, without overdoing, without going anywhere, much less "going against the grain." Like the cook in Step 43, she travels with the grain of Tao.

• May you have the opportunity to travel into the deep interior. May you be able to take what you experience there back out, into the world, and benefit yourself and others around you.

48

In the pursuit of worldly knowledge
every day something more is added.
In the pursuit of Tao
every day something is let go.
The sage does less and less
until he reaches the state of nonaction.
The sage does not act
yet there is nothing he does not achieve.
To be a ruler of all under Heaven
one must practice noninterference.
If one approaches things in this way
one may become a ruler of the whole world.

The Commentary

In this step, Lao Tzu makes the profound distinction between worldly, or book, knowledge and true knowledge. Every day we cram more knowledge, more experiences, and more useless thoughts into our heads—especially in the Internet age, when information is so easily accessed and so easily forgotten. But the person of Tao (*tao ren*) lets go of all of that. He clears out the useless knowledge so that he has room for true knowledge. Not only that, but day by day, he does less and less until he achieves true wu wei.

Traditional Chinese culture highly valued the role of the scholar. To be a scholar meant standing on one of the highest rungs of society. Young men spent many years taking examinations to gain positions in the government. The examinations were, in theory, open to any class of person. But in practice only rich families could afford the tuition for classes and the leisure for study. The exams drew on material from Confucian texts, and the students were not supposed to originate new thoughts; they were simply to regurgitate the knowledge that had been poured into them.

The exams were fraught with tension. Scholars who passed landed cushy civil service jobs and elevated not only themselves but also their whole family in society. With so much at stake, it is not a surprise to hear the many stories of young men who failed the exams and committed suicide. This is why Lao Tzu is adamant about not being caught up in this accumulation of useless knowledge.

Chuang Tzu, who brought Lao Tzu's teachings forward a generation, says:

> Tao is hidden behind partial understanding, and the meaning of our words is hidden behind a screen of flowery rhetoric. The great Tao is beyond words and beyond arguments. Great knowledge does not need words. The one who can speak without words and can know the Tao that cannot be named—this is called the Treasure House of Heaven.[1]

A sage is one who perfects living in wu wei. It may appear that he is doing nothing: he does not rack up accomplishments, accolades, or enviable positions. Yet, he achieves so much that is actually important. Instead of worldly achievements, he achieves self-cultivation, which is a much higher level of accomplishment.

THE PRACTICE Letting Go

Decreasing useless knowledge means decreasing the thoughts in our mind, especially in our meditation practice. In order to still our minds for deep meditation, we must let go of the thoughts that run through our head like wild horses. This includes thoughts *about* those thoughts. When we practice "tranquil sitting," we should devote many sessions to letting go.

Choose one of these instructions to work with as a guide in a session.

- Let go of the desire to attain anything from your tranquil sitting practice.

- Let go of the image of who and what you are that you have built up over the years.

- Let go of needing approval and reward from the outside world.

- Let go of your inner critic, or inner parent, who nags and disapproves.

- Let go of the need to be right, the need for approval, and the need to be rewarded.

- Let go of all your ideas of what a spiritual, or enlightened, person is like.

Each moment is a gift, an opportunity, and a chance to let something go, to empty our heads and open our hearts to the celestial mind that dwells within all. Then we can experience what is important in life: it's not how much we "know," but how much we understand.

---

1. Solala Towler, *Chuang Tzu: The Inner Chapters* (London: Watkins Publishing, 2010), 32.

49

The sage does not follow
her own heart-mind
but follows the heart-mind
of the people as her own.
To the good people
she is good.
To the not-good people
she is also good.
To the trusting ones
she extends trust (xin).
As for the untrusting
she also extends trust.
To be virtuous is to trust.
The sage in the world
unites herself with the heart-mind of everyone.
The people lift their eyes and ears to her
and she brings them back
to their childlike hearts.

The Commentary

A sage, or self-realized one, puts the desires of the people around her over her own desires. She treats good and not-good people the same and extends trust to everyone, trustworthy or not. Only because her Te, or spiritual power, is so strong is she able to do this. Truly, she feels at one with all of life.

As described in Step 17, other people look to her for guidance and as an example. She inspires them to return to their childlike hearts, which is a return to the innocence and purity of their youth, when they were untouched by the troubles of the world.

She does this by extending her trust to others. By doing so, she makes them feel they are trustworthy. *Trustworthiness* is defined as "the quality of being authentic and reliable," much like a sage, or Authentic Person. The Chinese word for trust, *xin,* also means "truthful," "honest," and "faithful." By extending her trust, a sage extends truthfulness and honesty, thereby bringing out those qualities in the people around her.

How can we learn to trust ourselves in the way of the sage? And how can we extend that trust to others: the good and the not-so good? How can we be free and strong in spirit so we can do this?

Lao Tzu says the answer to all these questions is to follow our own heart-mind and, at the same time, to unite with others. Not stuck in our own opinions or ideas, we are open to those of others. We extend toward the people around us and, in doing so, awaken something in them: they want to open their own hearts to us and listen to what we have to say.

When we limit ourselves to our own ideas, opinions, and narrow understanding, we cut ourselves off from those around us. But if we open up to learning from others, whether good or not-so-good, we broaden our understanding of the world and experience a level of trust we didn't know was possible.

We open our heart-mind first to ourselves, and then to the people around us. Next, we build trust within ourselves, and then extend that to others. But we are only able to do this if we can also trust our own process, the inspirational teachings of masters of Tao, and the practices that lead us back to Source. The practice in this step helps with all of this.

THE PRACTICE   Becoming the Watcher

As Lao Tzu says in Step 13, only those who value their own well-being *equally* with the well-being of the world will be trusted with that world. Through deep meditation practice, we can begin to trust our higher self, our Tao nature. By letting go of opinions and judgments, toward both ourselves and others, we can taste the power that comes when we let go and let be.

Inner Watching

- As you sit on your cushion or your chair, breathe deeply and slowly and let the thoughts of the day flow past your consciousness as if watching a movie screen. This will help you remove yourself from thoughts and not identify with them.

- As thoughts flow past on the screen, feel how little they have to do with you. They flow by, while you are rooted and strong and in harmony with the world. Let this feeling permeate your being. Let it fill up all the dark and troubled parts of your self.

- Experience the "watcher," the part of your consciousness that lets thoughts and feelings go by without clinging or judging. By focusing on the watcher, you will have the power to distinguish whether you are attached to the thoughts flowing by. If you are not attached to any of them, so much the better. And if attachment arises, watch it along with the rest of the movie.

- Let your being fill with this experience of Tao: that flavorless, soundless, indescribable nature of all that is, all that we are, and all that we will ever need.

- When you are finished, open your eyes and smile.

Outer Watching

- Sit outside on a chair or lie on the ground. Look up at the sky.

- Watch the tops of trees dancing in the breeze.

- Watch clouds floating by. Notice the shapes they take on, allowing your imagination to run free as you see things like animals and castles.

- Then watch the clouds pass, without any conceptual overlay. Just sit or lie there, observing clouds rolling by and trees dancing in the breeze, without any opinion about the experience or any need to force anything to be other than what it is.

- Try this meditation with a river, a lake, ocean waves, a candle, or campfire.

Inner and outer watching will help you become more objective and detached, less charged about your life and the challenges or frustrations that come up within it.

50

In *coming in* (being born)
and *going out* (dying)
those who follow life
are three in ten.
Those who follow death
also number three in ten.
Those who are living
yet moving toward death
are also three in ten.
Why is this?
Because most people
use up their lifeforce (chi).
Those who know how to
maintain their lifeforce
encounter no dangers on their way.
They can fight in a battle
and not be harmed by weapons.
They have nowhere for the rhinoceros
to stick his horn.
Tigers can find nowhere
to use their claws.
No weapon can harm them.
Why is this?
Because they have no place
for death to enter.

The Commentary

The world is full of people being born and dying—yet it seems that the majority of people are only moving toward death. Why is this? Through the way they live, they use up vital lifeforce (chi) without replenishing it and, therefore, move ever closer to death. Chi animates all of life; once chi is gone, there is no more life.

This is why people who manage their chi well do not face the same dangers. They can engage the battles of life and not be harmed. Because these people nourish and maintain their life energy, even wild animals cannot harm them. With strong lifeforce, the challenges of life—which Lao Tzu describes as weapons of war, rhinoceros tusks, and tiger claws—cannot harm them.

Chi needs to be nurtured and maintained so life can flourish. Many people squander chi by living unhealthy lifestyles, eating unhealthy food, thinking unhealthy thoughts, and flailing about in unhealthy emotional states. Their stock of chi gets used up, and, unless they do self-cultivation practices, their lifeforce depletes, which leads to death. On the other hand, people who live healthy and balanced lives live long, prosper, and feel happy. While serious illnesses can be karmic and therefore can strike people who live healthy lifestyles, for the most part, people who live in balance live longer and more happily.

If we eat foods that have no chi, they cannot produce or strengthen chi in our body. If we lead a stressful lifestyle, we will not be healthy. This can have its causes in anything from abusing drugs and alcohol to allowing our emotions to fluctuate wildly. While many health problems, including emotional ones, can be addressed through Chinese medicine and self-cultivation practices, we need to pay close attention to what is going into our body so that what comes out, or is expressed, will be positive and healthy.

A diet of fast food has no chi in it and no nutrition for living well. In Taoist texts, there are many instructions to "avoid the grains," which points to a low-carb diet. Even if you are not allergic to wheat gluten, it is still a good idea to keep grains to a minimum, as grains are very hard to digest and even have some toxicity. For most people, it is best to eat a wide variety of plants and a moderate amount of meat.

In Taoist thought, emotions are seen as energetic states. When they are not balanced and harmonious, they stress and drain our lifeforce. Observe your emotions: Are you depressed or sad a lot of the time? Do you get angry at people or circumstances? Do you wake up in the middle of the night with panic attacks or even night sweats? Do you become overjoyed to an extreme, leading to hysteria?

Thoughts can also become toxic. Observe them carefully: Is your thinking full of complaints and fears? Does it tend to run in well-worn grooves? Do your thoughts race when you are trying to sleep or even relax? Are your thoughts cranky and cause you to feel irritable? Do you forget things? These are all signs of imbalances that lead to chi loss.

It is helpful to spend more time doing stillness and "stillness through movement" practices. As Hua-Ching Ni says, "The best nourishment comes from your relaxed, calm mind. If you eat good food, but have a troubled mind, the results will not be good."[1]

This step reminds us to take good care of our chi. Through lifestyle choices and cultivation practices, we will be safe from outside harm and will have a long and peaceful life—until it is our time to merge back into the infinite.

THE PRACTICE   Heavenly Dew

This practice helps with digestion, stimulates your brain, and nourishes chi throughout your being.

- To stimulate both your gums and brain, as you did in Step 2, tap your teeth together thirty-six times, slowly and gently. All the teeth can touch at once, or you can do it nine times with the front teeth, nine times with the back teeth, nine times on the right, and nine times on the left.

- Next, exercise your tongue, which is called Turning the Red Dragon. Do this by circling your tongue all along the inside of your mouth, with lips closed. Start on the left and move to the right twenty-one times. Then circle from right to left twenty-one times.

- When you are finished, you should have a lot of saliva in your mouth. Taoists call this Heavenly Dew because saliva contains beneficial things like hormones, proteins, and other substances with digestive, mineral-building, and antibacterial functions. Swallow the Heavenly Dew either all at once or in three parts—making a gulping sound as you do.

- Visualize the saliva going all the way down to your lower dantian.

- While doing other practices, if you keep the tip of your tongue on your upper palate, you will also produce a lot of Heavenly Dew. You should swallow it in the same way.

---

1. Hua-Ching Ni, *8,000 Years of Wisdom,* Volume 1 (Santa Monica, CA: SevenStar Publications, 1983), 183.

51

Tao gives birth to all beings.
Virtue (Te) nurtures them.
Primal chi gives them shape.
Circumstances complete them.
Therefore the ten thousand beings
honor Tao and esteem virtue.
Tao is respected and virtue is honored
naturally and spontaneously (tzu ran).
Therefore we say that Tao
gives birth to all beings
and that virtue nurtures them,
nourishes them, and lets them grow;
raises them and allows them to ripen;
sustains them and protects them.
It gives birth but does not possess,
benefits but does not make claims,
develops but is not dominating.
This is called *profound virtue.*

The Commentary

Yes, all things come from Tao, but it is Te that nurtures them. Because Te is Tao made manifest, it makes us who and what we are. All the ten thousand beings—all of life on Earth—are manifestations of Tao, with Te giving them form and substance. Te can be thought of as the function of Tao in the world.

Primal Chi (*yuan chi*) gives them shape. Primal Chi is the basic life-force of the universe. As Hua-Ching Ni points out:

By understanding that all things in the universe are different expressions of chi, one can see why the sages have always said, "All things are one, and the one is all things." Without the outreach and withdrawal, the giving and returning of chi, the transformation of all things would be impossible.[1]

In the physical world, as well as the spiritual world, both Tao and Te are to be honored and esteemed. This is done naturally and without forethought (tzu ran or *ziran*), not to praise or supplicate but because it is natural to do so.

If we go against nature, or what is natural, we end up in trouble. If we go against our own nature, we suffer. Understanding this is called Profound Virtue (*xuan de*). As in Step 10, the word *xuan* can mean "dark," "mysterious," or even "magical" and indicates very deep understanding.

This idea of tzu ran is a fascinating one. It can mean "natural," "spontaneous," and "things as they are." Step 25 taught that humans follow nature, nature follows Tao, and Tao follows its own nature (tzu ran). This is why tzu ran can be associated with Primal Chi, as it is in this step.

If Tao is the source and destination of all life and if tzu ran means being true to our essential nature, the result is that we act spontaneously yet naturally—Chuang Tzu's "free and easy wandering." This is a way of living and relating with complete honesty and openness.

We can feel nervous about acting spontaneously because we worry we will attract too much attention or that others will judge and criticize us. Just remember that being spontaneous is not the same as acting out, just as having childlike delight or childlike innocence is different from being childish. Real tzu ran, or true spontaneity, happens when we act from our own deep nature, our Tao nature. This is not something that can be learned; it can only be experienced when the time is right, enough cultivation has been done, and we feel comfortable in our skin and our essential nature.

THE PRACTICE Living from Your Childlike Heart

A sage always acts from her childlike heart. Students often try to emulate it but end up embarrassing themselves because it is not genuine.

These tips will help you live from your own, unique childlike heart.

- As you do things, forget any agenda you may have.

- Act and communicate with your intellectual mind disengaged.

- Don't worry about whether you are doing things "right."

- Take chances.

- Keep your heart open. Keep your eyes open. Breathe from your belly.

- Imagine you are an innocent child approaching decisions and people as if you were experiencing everything for the first time.

- Let your spirit float outside the walls of your mind and be like a child dancing, not caring how you look to others, not caring whether you are doing it "right." Just enjoy your own being and animal body.

Dedicate one day a week to doing everything, and interacting with everyone, from your childlike heart. You can even prepare the people in your life by telling them what you are doing beforehand, in case you don't get it quite right. A spiritual practice like this brings joy to your life, delighting your heart and giving you wings for flying into the infinite.

---

1. Hua-Ching Ni, *Ageless Council for Modern Life* (Santa Monica, CA: SevenStar Communications, 1991), 1.

52

All beings under Heaven have an origin

which is the Mother of all things.

To know the Mother is to know her children.

To know her children

yet to be connected with the Mother

is to live to the end of one's life without harm.

Shut your mouth, close the door of your senses

and you will live long with no troubles.

If you keep interacting with the world

seeking to control it

and leaving the sense gates open,

you will be lost.

Perceiving the small is called *illumination*.

Preserving the soft and yielding is called *strength*.

Use the light to return to inner light.

In this way, you will not invite disaster

and will enter the eternal.

The Commentary

In this step, Tao is referred to as the Mother of all things. To know our source, the Mother, we need to know her children: us. To know ourselves is to be connected to the cosmic Source. When we experience a deep connection to this Source, we live without harm, are able to dance with change, and can flow with the challenges and opportunities life brings our way.

To do this, Lao Tzu offers more instruction for deep meditation, or stillness practice. By closing our mouth and shutting the door of our senses, we enter this meditation and live a long life with fewer troubles than someone whose sense doors are constantly open and overwhelmed by the ways of the world. People of the world, who never spend quiet time going within, become victims of their projections, fantasies, and perceived threats or wrongs. Seeking to control the world outside themselves cuts them off from the real world within. They lose the all-important connection to the Mother.

If we want to understand who and what we are, we need to take the time for the small moments of life. Life is not made up of one grand adventure after another; rather it is a succession of ordinary moments. In the same spirit of appreciation, we all have personal cycles: sometimes we're up, other times we're down. While we enjoy our high cycles much more than our low ones, we often learn much more from our low cycles. By honoring them and paying close attention to what they have to teach us, we become wise. To understand and cherish the small and the low is called *illumination,* which also translates as "lit from within."

Lao Tzu is offering us a practice of "turning the light around," in which the light of attention is turned onto the original mind consciousness. By allowing the light of awareness to penetrate the dark recesses of our mind, our true essential self—or Tao nature—emerges. Because we no longer identify solely with our own intellectual and energetic constructs, we become able to differentiate what is real from what is false, what is eternal from what is passing. The more fully a practitioner lets go of mental attachments, the more assistance comes his way—on spiritual and energetic levels. Taoists call this the *ming shen,* "radiant mind," or "radiant spirit."

The practice of Turning the Light Around is best offered in *The Secret of the Golden Flower* (*Taiyi Jinhua Zongzhi*), a text written by the famous immortal Lu Dong Bin. The book gives instructions on how to gather and refine our original spirit through the images of gold as the light of the original spirit and of the flower as the awakening—or blossoming—of that spirit.

THE PRACTICE   Turning the Light Around

This practice turns our attention inward so that we can arrive at the original mind, "the mind within the mind," the Source, our Mother.

- Sit on a cushion or on the edge of a chair. It is important to keep your body erect, without being stiff.

- Imagine there is a thread coming from the bai hui, the top of your skull, up to the Heavens, that is gently holding up your head.

- Place the tip of your tongue on the roof of your mouth and breathe slowly and deeply into your lower dantian.

- Close your eyes completely or leave them open just a little, focusing on the tip of your nose.

- Allow your thoughts to slow down until you can keep one thought, following the ancient instruction for entering a tranquil state: "Substitute ten thousand thoughts with one." This means that, instead of letting the wild horse of thought run all over your consciousness, gently guide him onto one path—and keep him there.

- One way to do this is to focus on your breath. Count each inhale and exhale as one breath, and keep counting up to ten or even higher—though it is better not to count more than thirty-six breaths. Allow your breath to become so natural and unforced that it is as if you are not consciously breathing anymore, but are instead "being breathed." This will help your mind become quieter, less active, and slower moving. It is not necessary to kill the wild horse—you only want to tame it. The more you quiet your mind, the more peaceful your spirit (shen) will become.

- Now turn your sight inward. Put all focus on your inner self; let go of your outer self. The outer world can be so distracting that, for most people, it has a strong hold on them even when they are meditating. Now is the time to let all of that go and turn your gaze away from the world, into your deep inner self.

- Allow the light of your inward gaze to connect you with your original spirit. Ever deepen your gaze and relaxation, noticing what arises in your experience. Spend at least twenty minutes in this state, so that it takes root in your being.

- To end this practice, as before, rub your hands together thirty-six times and then rub them up and down your face.

- Open your eyes. Sit still for a few moments to gather yourself before reentering the outer world of "doing" after spending time with "being." Don't just jump back into your day; instead enter it slowly. Because you may feel sensitive as you emerge, avoid any kind of emotionally disturbing communications for a while.

By practicing in this way, you will reach what Taoists call Living Midnight, a state of profound mental stillness and quietude that allows the original, or celestial, spirit to come forth.

If I possess any knowledge at all
I will walk on the great path of Tao
and my only fear will be straying from it.
The great path of Tao is very safe
yet people prefer to be sidetracked.
When the royal court is wasteful
the fields of the people become overgrown.
The storehouses are empty
yet the courtier's clothing is rich and brightly colored.
They wear sharp swords
and are full of drinking and eating.
They possess more wealth than they can use.
These people are like bandits.
This is not following Tao.

The Commentary

It is important, even crucial, to stick with our journey and not be sidetracked onto other pathways. There will always be glittering distractions in life that, unless we are vigilant, will pull us away from our journey. Ho Shang Kung says, "Great Tao is very smooth. But people love bypaths."[1] People try to take shortcuts in attempts to avoid hard work, but shortcuts lead far off the path, to dead ends, or may even get people lost, unable to find a way back.

The next part of this step can be read several ways. It can be a critique of the ruling class, who squander the wealth of the kingdom and force farmers—the bedrock of civilization—into penury. People go hungry while the ruling classes dress in fine silk, wear fancy weapons, and gorge themselves on fine food and drink. In essence, the ruling class consists of bandits, living off the people.

Another way to read these lines comes from understanding that the royal court can indicate spiritual practitioners who build up esoteric, intellectual, or mysterious riches, while ignoring the needs of those around them. Their fields are empty, which means their hearts and spirits are empty and uncultivated. While they show off their spiritual erudition, they have nothing of real value to offer. Their chi fields are also empty: they have squandered their jing and dress in bright colors to attract followers and attention. They show off the small skills they have learned in an ostentatious way, trying to gain glory and attention. Such people are not interested in serious self-cultivation; rather, they are after trivial powers in order to control others or make money. They stuff themselves with praise from followers and seek power and wealth.

According to Lao Tzu, such people are bandits. They may talk the talk, but they do not walk the walk. They may dress like spiritual teachers, but they do not have anything of value to teach. They may charge a lot of money to pass on their "knowledge," but it is empty knowledge. This is not Tao, Lao Tzu insists; this is not the true path.

It may be difficult—especially in the beginning—to discriminate false teachers from true ones. We need to stick to our own path and devote the time necessary for cultivating something that is long lasting. When false teachers offer shortcuts and easier paths, we must not fall for their traps.

This journey you are on is taken step by step and only *you* can walk your path. Only *you* can know what you need to do to reach your goals. Only *you* can resolve whatever karmic knots you have come here with to attain clear vision. Only *you* can move from ignorance to enlightenment. As Hua-Ching Ni asks, "The most important thing is: do you nurture and develop your own self-nature?"[2] Nothing else—career, health, relationships—is as important as that because everything falls into place once you are on your path, the one you were born to travel. This journey will take you many places; not all of them are pleasant, but they are all important to your spiritual growth—as long as you view them that way.

If you view painful places as problems, hassles, punishments, or judgments, you will suffer. While unavoidable in the world of dualism, you can learn to use suffering as impetus for growth, thereby reducing the pain you feel. Everyone suffers in this world, even sages, but they use their suffering as medicines, opportunities for growth, and as a way to deepen their self-cultivation.

THE PRACTICE Pain as Medicine

It would be great to learn solely from positive experiences. But when things are going well, we tend to neglect our self-cultivation practice and coast on good times. Then, when not-so-good times arise, we get angry, hurt, or frustrated.

The next time something causes you pain, try to view it as something offered to you from Tao. See it as a gift, not a punishment.

- The next time pain enters your experience, take a few moments to breathe.

- Take a few deep breaths and then relax your body.

- Take a few more deep breaths and then relax your mind.

- Take a few more deep breaths and then relax your nervous system.

- Take a few more deep breaths and then relax your chi, or energy body.

- Do not fight the pain and do not surrender to it, either.

- Follow the Watercourse Way and allow the pain to flow into you—and then flow out of you. Feel yourself flowing like water, endlessly adaptable and changeable, altering shape and direction as needed.

- Because water is ever-yielding, yet so powerful, it is all-conquering. Feel yourself merge with the endless flow of water that travels to the sea.

- Relax into the knowledge that you are flowing like water on your own sacred journey to the Source of all life, to Tao.

---

1. Eduard Erkes, *Ho-Shang-Kung's Commentary on Lao-Tse* (Zurich: Artibus Asiae Publishers, 1950), 94.
2. Hua-Ching Ni, *The Gentle Path of Spiritual Progress* (Santa Monica, CA: SevenStar Communications, 1987), x.

54

One who is firmly planted in Tao cannot be uprooted.

One who holds fast to Tao will not be taken away from it.

Grandchildren make offers to their ancestors.

Cultivate Tao in your being

and your virtue (spiritual strength) will be true.

Cultivate Tao in your family

and the virtue of your family will be strong.

Cultivate Tao in your village

and the virtue of your village will be long-lasting.

Cultivate Tao in the nation

and the virtue of the nation will be abundant.

Cultivate Tao with all under Heaven

and your virtue will pervade everywhere.

Contemplate oneness through yourself (*kuan*).

Contemplate the great family

through your own family.

Contemplate the great village of humanity

through your own village.

Contemplate the one nation

through your own nation.

Contemplate all under Heaven

to understand the whole world.

How do I know this to be true?

By listening to what speaks inside of me.

The Commentary

If we are firmly grounded in our practice, we will not easily be thrown off course. If we are serious about our cultivation of Tao, we will not lose it. The knowledge and experience gained by our cultivation efforts can be passed down to the next generation. Even if our children do not pursue Tao, they cannot help but be influenced in a positive way by our spiritual cultivation. If we cultivate Tao with our whole being, the Te of the sage will fill our bodies and hearts. We need to cultivate Tao in all aspects of our lives so that our own cultivation will blossom outward to affect those around us.

If we want to "save the world" or have any effect in the world around us, we must begin with ourselves. Then we extend, layer by layer, until we can truly influence our family, workplace, community, and even governing powers. Ho Shang Kung says, "Who cultivates Tao within his body, saves his breath, nourishes his spirits, augments his life, and accumulates his years. If his Te be such, then he will become a sage (zhen ren)."[1]

There is a sacred connection between our own heart and the hearts of all in our community. While it has long been a path of hermits and scholars, Taoism also has always "contained multitudes." Xuezhi Hu says,

> How many hearts are living in my own heart? One idea arises after another dies out. My ego exists as one among endless hearts (people), who lodge in my heart. So, to discipline my heart is the same as to discipline my endless peoples' hearts.[2]

While it important to maintain a feeling of community on a spiritual path, this can feel challenging for people who like to practice in solitude and keep to their own path. But we all need community—we all need to feel a sense of belonging within a family. This doesn't have to be our genetic family; it can be a community of spiritual-minded individuals gathered to exchange support and inspiration.

In this step, Lao Tzu describes how our own spiritual practice resonates up through the layers of our family, village, and nation—until we are all woven in a vast web of spiritual connections and attainment. We connect to this oneness of Source through ourselves. The term Lao Tzu uses is *kuan* (*guan*), meaning "inner observation" or "mystical vision," which also indicates a sacred site or a monastery. Taoist practices use the energy, or consciousness, of our body to bring us into an awareness that expands beyond it. By shining the light of awareness onto our body and our chi, we connect with what animates that body and energy system. We discover we are not limited by physical confines—our minds can go much further and our consciousness, or shen, can go even further.

While we want to feel connected to everyone, we need to start with a foundational Taoist principle: heal and strengthen ourselves first. We need to first know what is true. How do we do this? By listening to what "speaks" inside of us. But we will never hear that "still small voice" if our mind is too full of thoughts and desires. When we do listen with an open mind and open heart, we receive potent guidance and support.

THE PRACTICE   The Palace of Inner Observation

We practice this step by putting our attention into our body and then "forgetting" our body. Instead of following the mind, this meditation uses the practice of *chi kuan,* "observing the chi of our body." By paying attention to where chi flows strongly, where it is weak, and the places it is blocked, we can get a good picture of our energetic state.

- Sit or lie down in meditation posture. Close your eyes and allow your breath to become very slow and deep. Let your mind relax and let go.

- Feel awareness spread throughout your body. Breathe as you become aware of your body and what is happening within it. Do not judge, criticize, or force anything to happen.

- As your awareness, or consciousness, fills your whole body, bring the light of understanding to each of the five organ systems—then bring it to your whole body.

- Do not guide chi in any way; instead allow the information gathered by the observing awareness to flow through you. You can use it in your chi gong practice at a later time.

- A variation of this practice is to project your awareness outside your body and observe it from the outside. This can be described as "sending your heart outside of your body," with the heart center being our spiritual center and organ of discrimination.

- After a while, very slowly, so that you can really sense and experience each layer of being, allow the light of understanding to expand until it observes your whole family, whether genetic family or spiritual community.

- Then expand this to include your whole town or city.

- Then expand even further to include your whole country.

- And then, lastly, include all beings—all under Heaven.

- End your meditation by drawing your consciousness back through each layer, back to your own body—your own self. Whenever you want, you can recall the wonderful feeling of being connected with everyone on the planet in a vast spiral grid work, or spider web.

---

1. Eduard Erkes, *Ho-Shang-Kung's Commentary on Lao-Tse* (Zurich: Artibus Asiae Publishers, 1950), 95.
2. Xuezhi Hu, *Revealing the Tao Te Ching* (Los Angeles: Ageless Classics Press, 2005), 159.

55

The one who is filled with Te

is like a newborn baby.

Poisonous animals will not sting him.

Wild beasts will not attack him.

Carnivorous birds will not seize him.

His bones are weak

and his muscles are soft

yet his grasp is firm.

He does not know the union of man and woman

yet his penis becomes erect.

His lifeforce (jing) is so strong

he can cry all day without getting hoarse.

To understand true harmony

is to live in the unchanging.

To know the unchanging

is called *inner brightness* (ming).

To live only for one's self is called *inauspicious*.

When the desires of the mind

control the lifeforce

the result is *empty strength.*

Empty strength leads to exhaustion and decay.

This is not Tao.

What is not Tao

leads to an early death.

The Commentary

A person filled with Te, or spiritual potency, is compared to an infant, innocent and pure, who does not attract enmity from anyone or anything. An infant, despite soft muscles and weak tendons, has a firm grip. In the same way, students of Tao must have a firm grip on self-cultivation so they can practice the high art of wu wei—remaining soft, yet unwavering, on their path.

An erect penis without sexual energy and the ability to cry without getting exhausted or hoarse both show the strength of jing. An adult's erection depends on sexual stimulation, and it comes and goes. And any wailing would quickly weaken him and cause him to lose his voice within an hour.

Yet there is the true potency of the sage. True harmony arises from this potency, as we identify with not our limited, individual, ever-changing personality but with what is eternal and unchanging. To know this is ming, "inner brightness." When we are filled with Te, we become so pure and so strong that negative influences, which Lao Tzu symbolizes through poisonous animals, wild beasts, and carnivorous birds, cannot harm us.

Jing is both sexual and creative energy. When our jing is strong, we are radiant and attractive; when our jing is weak, we become impotent and dull-minded. Jing is one of the Three Treasures, (sanbao): jing, or "generative energy"; chi, or "vital force"; and shen, or "spirit." In nei dan, or internal alchemy practice, the practitioner transforms jing into chi and then chi into shen. Finally, shen is transformed back to Tao or wuji, the primordial. (You can see this process happening in the Diagram of the Great Ultimate, offered in Step 40.)

Jing is stored in our kidneys and is a finite resource, as it can be used up—which causes aging. If we take good care of our jing by eating well, treating our body well, and refraining from harmful sexual activity, we will age slowly and remain youthful until old age. But if we engage in harmful activities, we use up our jing and cannot replace it. We cannot create new jing; so we need to support the jing we have in a variety of ways. Movement practices, like chi gong, help jing a lot—especially if we do movements that work with kidney energy.

In Taoist sexual practices, men reduce ejaculation, thereby saving jing energy. They also guide sexual energy up their du mai channel, along the spine, which is a practice called "returning the essence to replenish the brain." (More information on this can be found in my book *The Tao of Intimacy and Ecstasy*.) Jing is also associated with yuan chi, or "Primal Chi"—the energy we receive from our parents at conception.

Problems with jing are indicated by childhood development issues, low sexual energy, and fatigue. Because all parts of the body are connected, low levels of jing will affect not only kidney-adrenal energy but also heart-spirit energy. Problems with heart-spirit energy, or shen, make themselves known through cognitive challenges, such as fuzzy thinking, memory loss, short attention span, insomnia, and absentmindedness.

THE PRACTICE Guarding the Jing

Temper Fire and Stimulate Water

Since jing resides in the kidneys, it has a water nature. The heart-spirit energy resides in the middle dantian and thus has a fire nature. There is another level of water within the fire as well. With stillness practice, we are seeking to discover the water that lies within the fire, thereby calming our mind or spirit. It is only by calming our mind and spirit that we can reach true harmony and experience what Lao Tzu calls the unchanging or inner brightness.

- Sit quietly on the edge of a chair or on a cushion. Close your eyes and breathe slowly and deeply through your nose.

- Send fire energy down to your lower dantian by placing your attention there.

- Feel the fire of your overactive mind be tempered by the calm waters of your kidneys.

Warming the Kidneys

This simple practice will fortify and energize our kidneys and is especially important to do in winter when kidneys are weakest.

- Rub your palms together briskly at least thirty-six times and then place them on your kidneys—in your lower back.

- Breathe warmth from your hands (lao gong) into your kidneys.

- Then, rub your hands in a circle, up the center of your back and out to the sides, at least thirty-six times.

Tips for Guarding the Jing in Your Life

When a restless mind controls lifeforce, we feel exhausted and express only empty strength. To avoid becoming a hungry ghost—perpetually unsatisfied with life, as Lao Tzu describes in Step 60—here is a list of things that help.

- Stillness practice

- Mindfulness practice

- Good old-fashioned temperance—that is, you don't have to follow each thought or desire to the end

- Paying attention to your higher self

- Centering yourself in your lower or middle dantian

- Anything that slows down your mind chatter

- Stillness through movement (tai chi or chi gong)

- Remembering your goal of becoming an awakened being

- Reading good books on spiritual teachings

- Living a simple lifestyle

- Not drinking alcohol—as it disturbs the spirit and the liver

- Reducing caffeine—as it disturbs the nervous system

- Making good choices in diet, exercise, sexual practices, and what you choose to put your mind on

- Not dwelling on your problems too much

- Being in nature on a regular basis

- Beginning your day with thoughts of gratitude

- Dedicating the fruits of your practice to others

- Bringing in the beautiful energy of sharing with others—which invokes the sweet feeling of dedicating your self-cultivation to everyone who dwells in painful states of suffering and ignorance

- Feeling the blessings and joy that come from sharing the deep healing of inner cultivation

56

The one who knows does not speak.

The one who speaks does not know.

Go within and retreat from the world.

Blunt your sharpness,

separate your entanglements,

soften your light,

unite with the dust of the Earth.

This is called *primal union*.

Do not concern yourself with friends and enemies.

Maintain your own center in the midst of activity.

Not concerned with good or bad, honor or disgrace

the sage is honored under Heaven.

The Commentary

This step begins decisively by saying that the one who knows does not speak and the one who speaks does not truly know. Many people trumpet spiritual achievement on the Internet or in various publications, but the more people talk about achievements, the less likely it is that they have actually achieved anything. A true Master of Tao does not trumpet achievement to the world, because the title is earned, not self-bestowed. A true Master embodies teachings in his being. Ho Shang Kung translates the second line of the verse as, "The knowing one esteems deeds and not words."[1]

He advises, "Though you may possess the enlightenment of unique insight, you must harmonize it. Let it become obscured; do not let it radiate."[2] So we go within and retreat from the world of form, separate from entanglements with the world, and become humble enough to "unite with the dust of the Earth." This union in humility is called "primal union" or "union with the dark one"—xuan. It is union with the very source of our being.

By not being concerned with the duality and its friend/enemy, good/bad, honor/disgrace dichotomies, and by maintaining our center in the midst of the activity, we can become a true sage, honored under Heaven.

THE PRACTICE   Stillness in the Midst of Activity

To maintain our center in the midst of activity is challenging, as the activity of the world tends to draw us away from our center. It is one thing to rest in a calm and centered state when we retreat into stillness or movement practices; it is quite another thing to maintain it during the stress of engaging with daily life.

For this practice, you will not sit on your cushion. Instead, you will take a small "time-out" in the midst of the activity.

- In the midst of your daily life, occasionally stop whatever you are doing and allow yourself to disconnect from it—though not while driving!

- Take a step back, energetically and emotionally, to enter a deep state of relaxation and contentment.

- Separate from your entanglements with the environment and spend a few precious moments in the even vaster world that is within you.

- Close your eyes, slow your breathing, and sink your attention down into your heart center or your lower dantian.

- Let go of fears and worries about the future to spend time in the endless present.

- Don't concern yourself with achieving anything in this small practice. Just allow yourself to enter a state that feels protected from the sharpness of the world, that unites you with the humble Earth under your feet.

- This state, called "primal union," will reenergize and balance your energy very quickly. Do this practice whenever you have moved away from your center, your shen. Don't just do it when you feel stressed—even when joyful and creative, it is good to take a small "time-out" to recharge, ground your energy, find balance, and therefore ward off hysteria.

- Because you are not concerned with achieving anything, this practice leads to deeper focus and the ability to maintain that focus in your daily activities.

Each moment of resisting the allure of the world of duality is a moment when we can add another brick of self-cultivation to our being.

---

1. Eduard Erkes, *Ho-Shang-Kung's Commentary on Lao-Tse* (Zurich: Artibus Asiae Publishers, 1950), 99.
2. Ibid.

57

Use justice to rule a country.
Use cunning when conducting war.
Use inaction (wu wei)
to master all under Heaven.
How do I know this?
Because of this:
When there are too many rules and regulations
the people become poorer.
When people have too many weapons
the country is in disorder.
When people resort to trickery and cunning
strange things begin to happen.
When there are too many laws and restrictions
there are more thieves and outlaws.
The sage-ruler does not act (wu wei)
and people transform themselves.
He dwells in tranquility
and people naturally become honest.
He does not interfere in the lives of the people
and they become wealthy.
He has no desires
and the people become natural (pu).

The Commentary

Ruling a country and waging a war use different sets of skills; so does living in the spiritual world while also living in the material world. We need to develop skills to move in every role and realm. Here we receive advice to apply wu wei as the method for self-mastery in the midst of it all.

It is possible to live as if in the mountains, away from the distractions of the world, right in your own home. This lifestyle includes regular meditation for inner journeying, physical and energetic practices such as tai chi or chi gong, and studying and applying teachings from ancient and contemporary masters. You can be a "mountain person" (*shanren*) by being strong, grounded, and solid—like a mountain—in your everyday life.

When there are too many rules and regulations, we become poorer, our spirit becomes rigid, and our chi is blocked. When people use weapons on each other, whether physical or emotional, everyone's hearts become disturbed. When we use trickery to navigate relationships, strange things happen that don't feel right or true. When too many laws restrict personal and spiritual life, people become outlaws, thieving to get what they need.

The true sage-teacher, or sage-ruler, does not lay down a long list of rules and regulations. Rather, his support allows his students or subjects to change of themselves. His tranquility inspires people to be honest, and by encouraging freedom, their lives become enriched. Without an agenda, his students evolve naturally.

As students of Tao, we can also evolve naturally. By remaining tranquil and calm in our heart, things naturally go our way. Other people notice and, unconsciously, treat us better. We even begin to influence those around us for the better. Not run by desires, we suffer less. Our hearts are lighter, our spirits grow brighter, and we begin to feel ease in all we do.

When we emphasize what is wrong in our lives and the world, our heart gets blocked, our spirit sinks, our mind becomes full of wildly racing thoughts, and our health declines. While no one wants to suffer, suffering is a part of everyone's life. So is the joy we crave.

Therefore, how can we eventually become a positive influence in such a negative world? Chuang Tzu says, "The sage of old cultivated himself before he attempted to help others. If you yourself are not cultivated, what help could you possibly be for others?"[1]

THE PRACTICE   One Thing at a Time

When we try to multitask, our focus is dispersed and we end up doing things partly well—and nothing perfectly. Consciously doing one thing at a time brings focus and balance to our heart-mind.

Here are ways to experience these benefits.

- Do an at-home retreat. Every once in a while, take a few days off from the world. Turn off the phone and unplug the computer, stock up on food, and spend your time quietly doing reflection, study, and cultivation practices. Tell roommates or family that you will neither initiate, nor respond to, any talking. You will be amazed by how deep you go and how much you benefit.

- When eating, only eat. Bite and chew slowly so you really enjoy the taste and texture of your food.

- When driving, only drive—don't talk on the phone.

- In your thoughts, dwell in the present moment rather than in the past or the future.

- It's okay to play music while working, exercising, or driving—just be sure it helps you focus on your task.

- When you have a conversation, focus on what the other person is saying rather than on what you intend to say next.

- At various times of each day, pay attention to your breathing and make sure to breathe deeply from your lower dantian. This will reduce stress, tension, and fear.

- Be true to your own natural (pu) self—do not force yourself into someone else's idea of who you should be.

- While practicing chi gong or tai chi, let each movement grow out of the movement before it. Then allow the movement to flow into the next so that they are all connected, like the brushstrokes that make up a beautiful painting.

- The next time you eat a piece of fruit or chocolate, let each bite slowly fill your taste buds with the food's essence—as if you had all the time in the world.

The truth is that you do have all the time in the world. Apply these "only one thing" practices throughout your day; you will be surprised by how much you can accomplish when not multitasking.

---

1. Solala Towler, *Chuang Tzu: The Inner Chapters* (London: Watkins Publishing, 2010), 70.

58

When the government's hand is light
people's lives are simple.
When the government has a heavy hand
people are clever and conniving.
Disaster may follow good fortune.
Good fortune may be hidden in disaster.
Who can tell the future?
Justice can turn into injustice.
Good turns into evil.
In this way, people are confused and lost.
Because of this the sage is sharp, but does not cut.
She is pointed, but does not stab.
She is straightforward, but does not overreach.
She is bright, but does not blind.

The Commentary

When powers that be rule with a light hand, people are at ease, so their lives are simple. But when rulers use a heavy hand to force people down, they respond as in Step 57, with cleverness, and they become conniving in order to circumvent the overbearing rules and regulations.

Lao Tzu reminds us that things constantly shift, change, and may not be as they seem. Disaster may follow good fortune—and disaster may be hidden in the guise of good fortune. We don't know whether we face justice or injustice from day to day, even moment to moment. What seems good today may seem evil tomorrow. Because of this, it is easy to become lost and confused.

Yet the sage is never lost or confused. The sage is sharply awake but does not harmfully cut others. Her awareness is a sharp point, but she does not stab anyone with it. In relationship she is straightforward but does not overreach—instead she practices wu wei. Although her inner light is strong, she does not blind others with it.

THE PRACTICE   The Hall of Light

This meditation works with the upper dantian—or third eye—and is sometimes called Celestial Meditation or the Hall of Light. This energy center is part of a greater grouping of points in the head, called the Nine Palaces (*jiu gong*). When we intentionally place attention here during meditation, we energize and stimulate this important point.

While this practice can be powerful to do in the evening, be sure to bring the energy back down to your lower dantian or feet; otherwise you may have trouble sleeping. As you start doing this meditation, first try it in the morning.

- Begin your meditation as usual, breathing deeply and slowly into your lower dantian. Keep your eyes closed so you can see with inner vision.

- Then raise your attention to the level of your third eye, which is in between your eyebrows and one inch inside your head.

- Breathe slowly into this area. Try to feel the depth of that point by sending your intention inside your brain.

- As you inhale, breathe golden light into this area.

- As you exhale, send red light out into the darkness of your spiritual ignorance, lighting the way for you to reach deeper understanding and insight.

- Feel this point opening. Feel how this affects other places in your energetic body, invigorating or healing them as needed.

- This place you are entering, the inner palace, is where transformation happens. It is where deep internal healing of the mind and heart happens. It is where you can be gifted with inner vision and the psychic perception.

- Spend some time in this important spiritual/psychic center. You may see colors, light, or other visions. Enjoy them but do not hold onto them.

- When you finish, bring your attention back down to your lower dantian. Never leave too much energy in your head, as it can cause insomnia or headaches.

- If you feel dizzy or have a "stuffed up" feeling in your head, bring your attention all the way down to the bottoms of your feet. You can also massage the bottoms of your feet, which is a great way to clear up any head-chi problems.

59

In cultivating yourself or

serving all under Heaven

it is best to use moderation.

Moderation is called *planning ahead*.

By planning ahead, one accumulates Te (inner power).

When one continuously accumulates Te

there is nothing that cannot be accomplished.

When there is nothing that cannot be accomplished

one knows no limits.

When there are no limits

one can rule a nation (one's own self).

If one is connected to the Great Mother

one can live a long life.

This is called *having deep roots*

and a solid foundation.

This is the Te of long life,

deep vision, and understanding.

The Commentary

Throughout the journey of self-cultivation, use moderation. Too much asceticism is as harmful as being too lax: don't be rigid and don't be lazy. Set your sight on the path in front of you and then follow that path, which is called "planning ahead."

With a deep connection to Tao as the Great Mother, we will live a long and healthy life. As Lao Tzu describes in Step 20, even though others may view us as slow or even stupid, we know in our heart that we are connected to a most precious Source that supports and nourishes us. This image of Tao as the great yin (*tai yin*)—as the valley spirit, the mysterious mare, and the Great Mother—is a powerful one. Because we feel nourished and supported by this Source, we have deep roots and a solid foundation. Therefore, our visionary understanding of both Tao and ourselves is complete.

Being rooted physically and emotionally helps us process our spiritual experiences when our feet are firmly on the path of Tao. If we are not emotionally stable, we can be thrown off-center and frightened when spiritual guides communicate with us or we receive downloads of spiritual chi into our body. Taoist practice takes us from a limited experience of the world to the world of the unlimited. This is when we become masters, or rulers, of our kingdom. If we maintain a deep connection with the Great Mother, our roots will grow deep into the Earth. This provides a solid foundation—spiritually, emotionally, and energetically.

To develop a deep connection to the Great Mother, we can learn from nature and work with the energy of trees. As Hua-Ching Ni teaches,

> Human life is conceptual; we learn from books and new ideas. Trees do not learn from ideas: they learn directly from reality. If anything changes, they immediately know about it. It takes humans much longer to discover a problem, but the trees know immediately.[1]

When most people picture a tree, they see a trunk with branches, leaves, and perhaps flowers or fruit; yet much of the mass of a tree is below the Earth in a root system that is often larger than what we see above ground. As spiritual travelers, we need the same strong root system a tree has—as Lao Tzu emphasized in Step 26. The energy of a tree can show us how to extend our own energetic root system deeply into the Earth. Then, in our cultivation practices, we can establish a strong root system of our own.

THE PRACTICE Tree Chi Gong

In this practice, we can develop our connection with nature and the living beings that surround us by connecting with, and learning from, a tree.

- Go to a tree that looks healthy and abundant. Stand with your back to it, resting on its trunk. Lace your fingers together in front of your lower dantian. Close your eyes and slow your breathing.

- As you breathe in, allow the chi of the tree to enter your body.

- Then, when you exhale, let all the tensions, toxins, disease, and pain flow out of you and into the tree. (Doing this will not harm the tree.)

- As you breathe in and out, feel the life form that the tree is and deepen how you connect your personal chi with the chi of the tree.

- Trees breathe in their own way, contributing to the rich oxygen that humans and all living creatures breathe every day. So once a connection is made, you and the tree can breathe together. Feel yourself breathing along with the tree, mingling your chi. This allows you to receive information about the kind of beingness that lives in the trees surrounding us.

- At this time, you can ground yourself, as you did in Step 26, mingling your roots with those of the tree.

- You can also send your chi down through the bottoms of your feet and into the roots of the tree below you.

- Then, instead of bringing your chi up the du mai in your back, as you have in other practices, send chi up the roots of the tree. Feel the chi rise up through the trunk, all the way to the highest branches.

- Now guide the chi from those branches into your bai hui point at the top of your head and then down the front of your body—your ren mai. Pull the chi down to your lower dantian.

- Stand quietly. Feel the chi running from your lower dantian down to your feet, down into the roots of the tree, up the tree trunk, and up to its highest branches, and then down through your bai hui, and all the way down to your lower dantian.

- Do this cycling of chi between nine and thirty-six times.

- To finish, turn to the tree and bow three times. At first, it may seem funny to bow to a tree. But—especially if the tree is large and healthy—the tree has not only its own chi but also wisdom that is just as real as that of any human sage.

---

1. Hua-Ching Ni, *The Gentle Path of Spiritual Progress* (Santa Monica, CA: SevenStar Communications, 1987).

60

Ruling a large country is like cooking a small fish.
Use Tao to approach all things under Heaven
and evil will have no power.
It is not that evil has no power
but its power cannot harm you.
Not only will its power not harm you
but the sage also harms no one.
When the sage and evil
do no harm to each other
virtue is unified and restored.

The Commentary

This is another teaching on wu wei or noninterference. When you cook a small fish, the less often you turn it, the less likely it is to fall apart. Of course, the image of "ruling a country" is also a description of ruling one's own inner landscape. It is important to take care of each detail of our cultivation (fish cooking), but at the same time, it is also important to not fuss too much. We know the path that is before us, and we know the practices it will take to get down that path. We have our map, and many wonderful and wise teachers have given us directions.

If we align ourselves with Tao, evil (negativity) will have no hold on us. It is not that evil itself has no power, we are told, but that its power cannot harm us. Not only will evil have no power over us, but as we become sages, we will not only bring no harm to others, but we will also serve as a conduit for Te, or spiritual virtue, to reside in everyone we meet.

Again, we see that the metaphor of ruling a country equates with taking care of our own country—our small self—so that we can cultivate our big self, or what the Buddhists call our Buddha Nature and

Taoists call our Tao Nature. Spending too much time trying to figure things out with our small mind will—like the overcooked fish—destroy the very thing we're tending.

The word used in lines three, four, and eight, which I have chosen to translate as evil or negativity, is *gui,* which can also mean "ghost" or "demon." In Chinese mythology, there is a figure called the "hungry ghost." These people live lives of greed and selfishness. After they die, they become ghosts with huge empty bellies, yet with necks so thin and mouths so tiny they can never fill their bellies, no matter how much they eat.

Many of us have encountered these hungry ghosts in our own lives, those people whose greed is insatiable. They always want to consume more—money, sex, power, and food. They try to devour those around them, in hopes that this will sate their hunger. We may even encounter very powerful people who, in reality, are hungry ghosts. But if we cultivate ourselves, we will not be harmed by them. They are just shells of people who are trying, in vain, to stuff themselves, even if it means feeding off the people around them. It is not that these people are not real, they are; but they cannot harm a person who has cultivated his or her spiritual power.

If you fear you are a hungry ghost, the best thing you can do is cultivate yourself as much as possible to allow your spiritual understanding to grow so that your greed will abate and you will develop into a real or authentic person (zhenren). It may take some time, even more than one lifetime, to really untangle the karmic debts that have turned you into a hungry ghost, but it can be done.

THE PRACTICE   Hungry Ghosts

When you encounter hungry ghosts in your life, remember:

- Taoists do not believe in "eternal damnation."

- Anyone can be saved.

- Anyone can grow spiritually and, through the grace of the Great Mother, can transform themselves from a greedy, gluttonous person to a person of grace and generosity.

- We have all the tools we need.

- We have a clear map to follow.

- We have guides who will assist us all along the way.

- No excuses! There is no reason not to try to evolve and transform.

- Don't be a thirsty, hungry ghost, always seeking to stuff knowledge, power, or experiences (even spiritual ones) down your tiny gullet.

- Be content to take in knowledge and experiences slowly, one bite at a time, one step at a time, and one moment at a time.

A great country is like the lowlands of a river,

where all things converge.

In this way it is the feminine nature

of the universe.

The feminine uses stillness

to overcome the masculine.

In stillness she takes the lower,

more humble position.

Thus the truly great nation

puts itself lower than the smaller nation.

In this way it gains dominion

over the small nation.

When a small nation

submits humbly to a great nation

it gains protection from the great nation.

In this way a country may use humility to gain

either dominion or protection.

A great nation's desire

should be to unite and lead its people.

A small nation's desire

should be to join with others.

For both nations to get what they desire

the large one needs to act with humility.

The Commentary

Hua-Ching Ni says it is the gentle, persevering, constant feminine virtue of the universal valley that manifests as the spiritual virtues of the subtle universal Source.[1]

Lao Tzu uses the image of the "valley spirit," describing it as the lowlands of a river valley. Taoists see both yin and yang but emphasize the true nature of the universe as being of a yin, or feminine, nature. While the yin position in any relationship may initially be seen as the lower or more humble one, it is actually the point of power. By recognizing yin energy as the more important, long-lasting energy, Taoists have always emphasized the power of stillness over movement. Even in Taoist moving practices, there is always a place of stillness within. Some teachers describe this as the "water within the fire."

Step 61 is usually translated as a primer on international relations, but we can also see it as directions on how to relate to the people around us. People in a position of power or authority can be likened to a large country, while those in a lesser position can be seen as a small country. When a person of lesser power or authority takes the yin position of being humble, the person of greater power is impressed and often becomes less dominant in order to give the person of smaller power room to grow. By not attacking or pressing forward, the "smaller country" ends up with more power.

The one who is truly great, the sage, puts herself below others, takes the smaller portion of authority, and remains humble and sincere. Thus, she receives greater recognition. Some people want to lead and give order, whereas some people prefer to work with others, thus becoming even more accomplished. This takes a special kind of humility.

Step 61 is easy to apply to everyday life and any kind of relationship—job, family, partnership, or marriage. If we work well *with* others instead of wanting them to work *for* us, we embody what Lao Tzu is talking about when he describes the large country and the small country. Often, when people find themselves in a position of power and authority, they act like big shots, lording it over those around them. Of course, no one likes to interact with someone like this. We may even know the job better than they do and be better at doing it, and so we may feel resentment toward them.

The Taoist advice is not to bang our own drum but to take a more humble attitude toward the person who is more powerful than we are. If we restrain ourselves and do our best to support and even assist that person, often he or she will respond more positively than if we just complained or undermined them. If, however, we find ourselves in a position of power, instead of lording it over others, we would do better to listen to those below us with sincere openness. This is true power, the power of the yin, of stillness and humbleness.

Sometimes we need to move ahead; sometimes we need to pull back. Sometimes we need to push ourselves a little; sometimes we need to give ourselves a break. Sometimes we need to take the lower, yin position, but sometimes we need to take the higher, yang position. There is nothing wrong with balanced yang or masculine energy, yet it is all too often an unbalanced version that we see. The problem with too much yang energy is that it is easy to begin projects, new jobs, and new relationships but often difficult to stick with them. This is why we need both yin and yang and why the Taoist emphasis is on the yin as a means to counterbalance what is seen as too much yang energy in the world.

Without the yin aspect to support and harmonize it, too much yang or masculine energy will cause problems, whether in the home, at work, or even between countries.

THE PRACTICE Balancing Yin and Yang

In Taoist practice, we honor the yin and the yang, the Earth and the Sun, the female and the male, quiescence and activity, inward direction as well as outward direction. We are all creatures of both yin and yang and need to have a healthy balance of both within our being. Staying with only yin or yang for "spiritual" reasons will cause an energetic/spiritual imbalance in our system.

Look within and determine which is the correct way to move:

- If you tend toward yang energy, the next time you feel the urge to move forward in a yang, masculine way (whether you are female or male), take a few moments to try to see it from another side, another angle—the yin perspective. Try to temper your fiery, creative yang with some of the watery wisdom of the yin. You may be surprised by how much more you will accomplish.

- However, if you tend to be a yin-oriented person, try creating some strong (yet balanced) yang in your life.

- Try not to overdo it.

- Try not to push forward while disregarding the feelings or the energy of those around you.

- In Taoism, we practice great and deep stillness as well as energetic and graceful movement. In this way, we honor our yin as well as our yang natures.

---

1. Hua-Ching Ni, *Mystical Universal Mother* (Santa Monica, CA: SevenStar Communications, 1991), 9.

62

Tao is the great mysterious source of all life.

The good person (sage) holds it close.

It is the shield of the bad.

Yet though fancy speech can buy high rank

and good manners buy high status,

let us not discard those who are not good.

When the emperor is crowned

and the three officials installed,

though they are accompanied

by many pieces of jade and horses,

this is still not as valuable as

aligning one's self with Tao.

Since ancient times

why has Tao been honored in this way?

It is said,

if you seek you will find.

If you have committed crimes

you will be forgiven.

In this way, Tao is honored above all else.

The Commentary

Tao is the source of all life and is described as a great mystery. "Good people" or virtuous people know they can reside in this great mystery and it will enfold them in its vast and beneficent embrace; yet "bad people," who may not be moral or virtuous people, are equally enfolded. We may rise in the material world through our own good graces, good karma, or just luck, but the poor, discarded, homeless people we see on the streets are just as worthy as we are of rewards.

In ancient times, when a new emperor was crowned, there was great celebration and solemn ritual. The crowning of the "three officials," who would be working closely with the emperor, was an important element of that ritual. Of course, much money was spent on this pageantry.

Yet, Lao Tzu tells us that aligning ourselves with Tao is of even greater importance. It has always been this way. If, with an open and humble attitude, we seek a deep connection with Tao, we will find it. If we wish to change our unfortunate or unvirtuous state, we can do that as well. What is of most importance is our relationship with the eternal.

In ancient China, punishment could be enacted on the whole family. Criminals, especially those convicted of treason, would have their entire family executed, often down through three generations. But in Tao, the virtuous and the not virtuous are all the same. For some people this may not seem right, as we think evildoers deserve punishment. No matter. In Tao we are all equal. Of course, evildoers may create a lot of difficult karma for themselves and may suffer because of it, but if they turn aside from evil and toward Tao, Tao will embrace them.

The "three officials" can also be seen as the Three Treasures, or san bao—essence or jing, vital energy or chi, and spirit or shen. The character for chi pictures a bowl of rice with steam rising from it. As we know, chi is the energy that animates all of life. Yet, there are many different kinds of chi. Even the weather is a kind of chi, and the food we eat gives us a kind of chi (*gu chi*).

There are two different basic forms of chi—the pre-Heaven (original or yuan chi) and the post-Heaven. The pre-Heaven is the chi we receive from our parents in the moment of conception and is said to begin with our first breath outside the womb. The post-Heaven is the chi we work with in our chi gong practice.

Shen, or spirit, also has two different forms—the precelestial (*yuan shen*) and the postcelestial (*houtian shen*). In nei dan, or inner alchemy, practice, one uses "embryonic" breathing to achieve a luminous state or yin spirit (*yin shen*). Further practice is needed to refine the yin spirit into a yang spirit, sometimes called the Golden Embryo or the Red

Baby, which leaves the body through the crown of the head (bai hui) and can live outside the body.

For thousands of years, Taoist aspirants have practiced developing each of the Three Treasures into their highest states. And even though the world we live in has changed immeasurably from Lao Tzu's time, our bodies and energetic systems have remained the same. The practices that Taoists have been doing for all these millennia still work the same for us as for the ancient masters.

Yet even these essential practices are nothing if we do not align ourselves, in our deepest being, with Tao. It has always been this way, says Lao Tzu. If we seek union with Tao, the very act of opening ourselves up to it will allow that to happen. No matter how bad our past has been, if we truly seek union with Tao, it can happen.

THE PRACTICE   Clarity and Quiescence Practice

The practice of clarity and quiescence (*qing jing*) is considered the ideal state of body and mind. This is a very ancient idea, going at least as far back as the *Tao Te Ching*. It has had a lot of influence on later Taoist religious practices as well.

- Sit or lie down as in previous steps. Breathe very slowly and deeply, through your nose, with the tip of your tongue on the roof of your mouth.

- Allow your breath to slow down as much as possible, until your breathing becomes light and very, very deep.

- Feel your whole abdomen expand slowly as you inhale and then contract slowly on your exhale.

- Feel yourself opening like a flower.

- Expand your being and allow it to unfurl, just like a flower opening toward the sun.

- Feel your being opening toward the mystical Great Mother of Tao.

- Feel yourself enfolded in her arms, where you are safe, warm, and loved.

- As you continue to breathe slowly and deeply, allow yourself to feel your connection with Source.

- In those moments in life when you feel disconnected from this Source, allow yourself to drop back into this meditation until you feel connected again. In truth, we are never disconnected from Tao, though our experiences in the world may make us feel that we are.

- Stay with this meditation until you feel your connection with Tao as a strong bond, permeating every part of your body and spirit.

- Let your mind relax and release its hold on your energy body.

- Just sit and allow yourself to "be breathed."

- Permit yourself to become the beautiful flower that you are.

63

Practice nonaction or wu wei.

Accomplish without accomplishing.

Taste what has no taste.

The great comes from the small.

More begins with less.

Return bitterness with kindness.

Deal with the difficult while it is still easy.

Create the large from the small.

The sage does not try for greatness

and so he is great.

Promises made too lightly are hard to keep.

Easy tasks often become difficult.

The sage is always ready for difficulties

and for this reason never experiences them.

The Commentary

Here we have a recipe for living a full and long life. As usual, Lao Tzu is giving us the good advice to practice wu wei.

Everything great, Lao Tzu says, begins from something small. Of course, we can see this in nature, as even the mightiest tree begins as a small seed. So too will our cultivation practice bloom when we plant and tend our spiritual "seeds."

Don't make promises too lightly, says Lao Tzu. When we make promises, we need to be certain we will be able to follow through with them. This is an important teaching. We make promises to those around us all the time, often without even noticing. Whenever we say we will do something or we will be a certain kind of person, that is a promise. Whenever we begin a new project, we make a promise to ourselves or to the other people involved that we will follow through with it. Whenever we begin a new relationship, we make a promise that we will be honest with that person. Whenever we tell ourselves that we will do better in the future, be a better person, or do our practices more regularly—these are all promises.

Just as it is important that we not make promises too lightly to others, this applies even more so to ourselves. We can endeavor to always do our best, with the full understanding that what we mean by "best" may change over time or perhaps every day. Doing our best, even if we do not always succeed, aligns us with our Heavenly mandate and attracts assistance from the spiritual plane.

Our journey may take us over some rough roads. Sometimes we will feel that we are walking up an endless mountain trail, with steep cliffs on one side and an endless drop on the other. Other times we will feel like we are even walking in circles. This is all part of the journey; but if we make a conscious promise to do our best in each moment, we will reach the Source.

THE PRACTICE The Wu Wei
Way of Effortless Effort

The wu wei way comes up repeatedly in Lao Tzu's teaching. Sometimes wu wei means that instead of *not* doing something, we are actually *doing* something, but doing it in the right place and the right time. It can also mean *not* doing the things that we know are not good for us. This may seem like a simple practice, but it is often quite difficult.

Ask yourself: How do I know which things are good for me, and which are bad? Does wu wei mean not eating the foods that contribute to ill health? Does it mean not spending too much time in front of the television? Does it mean not working too hard, not sleeping too little, not eating too much, and not sitting around too much?

It can mean all these things and more. We already know, deep inside, what we need to do to maintain a healthy lifestyle, but our willpower is often very weak. We give in to urges when our energy is low, which often contributes to our energy weakening even further.

- The key to living a wu wei life is in going slowly or *manzou*.

- By slowing your actions, slowing your mind, and slowing your responses to outside influences or interactions with others, you will begin to live your life in harmony with wu wei.

- When you are quick to judge, quick to form opinions, quick to make snap decisions, quick to anger or be hurt—all these things will send you farther and farther away from wu wei.

- By slowing down, you are better able to perceive what is going on energetically in any situation.

- By moving slowly, you are less likely to be involved in accidents.

- By listening slowly, you are better able to really understand the other person.

- By taking the time to allow something small to grow into something big, you will be more likely to succeed in your endeavors.

- So, go slowly, be patient, be awake, be grateful, and do your best.

64

Peace is easily maintained.

What has not yet happened can be planned for.

The fragile is easily broken.

The small is easily scattered.

Act before small troubles become large ones.

Control problems before they become unmanageable.

The largest tree grows from a tiny shoot.

The highest tower is built brick by brick.

A journey of a thousand miles

begins with the first step.

To try too hard is to fail.

To grasp at things is to lose them.

This is why the sage does not force things.

In this way he is never defeated.

He does not grasp and so he does not lose.

Often people give up just on the verge of succeeding.

If one is as careful at the beginning

as at the end of any endeavor,

he will never be defeated.

This is why the sage does not desire

what the common people desire.

He does not value material things.

He does not study what others study.

He values what others have passed by.

He allows things to be what they are

without attempting to change them.

The Commentary

Peace can be maintained, but only by making the right choices.

Ho Shang Kung says: "The practice of asceticism and the government of the country are easy to keep for the restful one."[1] This image of "the restful one" is powerful. It describes those who are at peace within themselves. This is why, for them, peace is easily maintained. The restful ones make plans so that what they create will bear fruit.

They understand that the small and delicate can easily be broken, while the small or limited can easily be scattered or forgotten. If not acted upon, small troubles or problems have a way of becoming big ones. The sage takes care of problems while they are still small and manageable and therefore avoids bigger problems later on.

Huge trees, like huge problems or big projects, begin with a small seed. This can be a physical seed in the ground or an idea or inspiration. The tallest building must be built from the ground up. The longest journey begins with the first step.

Yet, if we lose sight of wu wei and instead practice *you* wei, or if we try to *force* things to happen, they often blow up in our face. If we grasp things too tightly, we will lose them before we can enjoy them. The sage, on the other hand, does not try to force or grasp; thus, what he creates is long lasting. He does not lose faith if his practice does not bring instant results. He does not desire what others desire; he does not value material things. What he values is not what the world values. He enjoys the world as it is without trying to change it.

Our journey, says Lao Tzu, begins right under our feet. It is accomplished by putting one foot in front of another. Momentum begins the journey, and momentum carries us through to the end. Ho Shang Kung explains this by saying, "Proceeding from what is near one reaches what is far away."[2]

It is by experiencing ourselves as "the restful one" that we are able to both begin and continue this journey. If we are restful inside, if we are peaceful inside, if we are accepting and engaged with the world as it is, without attempting to change it, we are more likely to not only enjoy our interaction with the world but also profit from it.

Therefore, we must use the mantra "pay attention." By paying attention to problems when they are small, we can avoid them becoming big. Also, if we pay as much attention to completing projects as we do to beginning them, we will be more successful. If we pay attention, plant our seeds deep in the Earth, and take good care of them, they will grow into beautiful flowers.

We pay close attention to the subtle and sublime works of nature and the natural world rather than to the gross and commercial aspects of the world. We pay attention to what others miss because they are moving too fast; are looking down instead of up; are deadening their senses with drugs, alcohol, and unhealthy food; are wasting their chi on egoistic struggles; or simply cannot imagine a world outside of the physical one they engage every day.

Our journey toward Tao will bring us to places and feelings of which we did not even know we were capable. It will show us amazing and magical things and will constantly surprise and excite us. It will, ultimately, allow us to expand our sense of being and of self and allow us to experience ourselves as the sages we truly are. But we must pay attention! This, of course, involves slowing down, as do most Taoist practices. It also involves concentrating on each step. Yet, while we are paying close attention to where we are placing our feet, we must also be sure to "look up" at the same time.

It is through this paying attention, this not grasping, and this looking up that we are able to become what the Taoists call an immortal or xianren. A xianren is "a person who has attained immortality and may possess supernormal powers such as the ability to fly."[3] Another translation of *xianren* is "a transcendent," or someone who has transcended the Earthly or material plane (di) and is able to fly to the Heavens (tian). This kind of person is often described in Taoist writings as being able to fly off into the clouds on the back of a dragon when life ends. Chuang Tzu describes this kind of person like this:

Here was such a one that could not be moved by flattery or praise. Nor would he be moved if the whole world should find fault with him. This is because he knew the difference between what was inner power and what was outer power; he knew the difference between what was true honor and what was true disgrace. But suppose we could ride upon the energy of Heaven and Earth and the six transformations of chi, then we could wander endlessly throughout the world and beyond.[4]

THE PRACTICE   Looking Up Practice

To engage the practice of looking up, remember these tips:

- When walking, be aware of where you are putting your feet, but at the same time, don't forget to look up.

- As you traverse the Earth, pay attention to what is floating above you.

- See the blue sky, the billowing clouds, or the sunshine shining down on you.

- Or enjoy the dark rainclouds and the rain itself, dancing down upon you.

- Watch the beautiful dancing of the birds as they swoop and fly overhead in unison or one by one.

- If you go through life with your head down (both physically and energetically), you will miss so much of the magic that happens all around you.

- This also means paying attention and taking in the "big picture" of your own life.

- You may get so bogged down in the minutiae of your day-to-day existence that you lose sight of what is really going on in your life.

- You may become so distracted by the small picture of what is going on in any one moment that you don't realize that you cannot see the grand mosaic of your life being revealed.

- It is when you look up that you are better able to look within.

- Lao Tzu tells us that we may suffer because we have a limited sense of self. It is in the act of looking up and then looking within that you are able to transcend this limitation and see yourself as the grand and greater being that you truly are.

- Why not leave your petty problems behind and open yourself to growth, insight, and spiritual evolution?

- Why not learn to stretch your wings and become a "cloud wanderer"?

- Why not learn how to fly on the back of a dragon?

1. Eduard Erkes, *Ho-Shang-Kung's Commentary on Lao-Tse* (Zurich: Artibus Asiae Publishers, 1950), 111.
2. Ibid.
3. Miura Kunio, *The Encyclopedia of Taoism* (New York: Routledge, 2008), 1092.
4. Solala Towler, *Chuang Tzu: The Inner Chapters* (London: Watkins Publishing, 2010), 121.

65

In ancient times rulers knew how to follow Tao.
They did not try to enlighten (ming) the people
but kept things simple.
People are difficult to rule
if they are too clever.
If the ruler tries to use too much cleverness to rule
the country will be full of thieves and brigands.
Those who try to use too much cleverness
to rule the country will not succeed.
Understanding these two principles
is called *profound virtue.*
Profound virtue is deep
and far-reaching.
It enables all things to return to Tao
and leads to great harmony.

The Commentary

Again, we can use the image of the ruler of a country as a sage ruling her own inner kingdom. In the previous steps, Lao Tzu uses the character *ming* as illumination or self-knowledge, but here there is a different character for *ming* that stands for "the light that makes us self-conscious and stand apart from others."[1]

This description of a state of self-consciousness is not what Lao Tzu and other ancient teachers sought. Indeed, too much emphasis on "enlightenment" can be a barrier to the enlightenment process. Keeping things simple and not emphasizing a goal has long been a tradition of Taoist teachers, apparently ancient even in Lao Tzu's time.

Lao Tzu's work is very simply written. He was following the paths of the ancient teachers who knew how to keep the teachings simple and easy to follow without forcing students to jump through too many hoops in order to "get to the real teaching." In this way, students of Tao don't have to be "clever" or resort to tricks of one kind or another to get to the "good stuff," and the teachers do not have to use cleverness or trickery with the students. This leads to a healthy relationship between teacher and student.

This absence of forced cleverness is called "primal virtue." Lao Tzu uses the word *xuan* here again. As previously mentioned, this can mean dark, mysterious (as used in Step 1), primal, subtle, profound, arcane, or even wondrous. This kind of deep understanding of the nature of the universe is so deep and far-reaching, it enables anyone who has attained it to "return to Tao."

Much of Taoist practice is about returning—returning to that primal state of complete naturalness and oneness with the world around and within us. This can, of course, take a lot of time and practice. Yet the teachings of Lao Tzu are very simple; he does not map out a lot of complicated practices. The principles of wu wei, Watercourse Way, valuing "belly" knowledge over "head" knowledge, breathing into dantian, stillness in movement—these kinds of things are easy to understand. Of course, putting them into practice is another thing.

The term *zhenren* (authentic or self-realized person) is related to the term *shengren* (sage or saint). Another related term is *shenren,* meaning divine or holy person. These all describe the one concept of the sage who, by her self-cultivation practice, has attained a high level of being. However, even in that high attainment, this sage can often pass unnoticed by others. What kind of a person is able to pass unnoticed by others? Lao Tzu describes her as wearing rough or plain clothing on the outside while carrying jade (wisdom, spiritual knowledge) in her heart. At times she appears dull or even stupid. She is seen as nothing special and teaches without using words. Yet, at the same time, people are drawn to her and love being in her presence. She is able to inspire, instruct, and illuminate others by her very being.

This is a little of what Lao Tzu means when he says that the true teacher does not try to "enlighten" students or make them feel self-conscious and apart from others. She does not use cleverness and trickery to teach others; instead, she keeps her teachings simple and easy to apply.

Everything in Lao Tzu's book can be applied to our everyday life. Everything he teaches or describes is useful. Yet sometimes it is by what he *leaves out* that we learn the most.

THE PRACTICE   The Journey to Wholeness

This journey we are on to wholeness, happiness, and a deep understanding of the universe and our place in it can be challenging, frustrating, awe inspiring, and deeply satisfying, but only if we truly take the lessons to heart and apply them to our own lives. We can travel it only if we reach beyond what we see right in front of us and look deeply into not only our own heart but also the heart of the world. Each practice, each principle, each step along the way can be a step of joy and expansion, of excitement and enjoyment. Each lesson we learn can be another doorway into a vast world of knowledge and attainment, the Gateway to All Marvelous Wonders, but only if we pay attention, only if we wake up from our dull dreams, only if we choose the path of knowledge and wisdom, only if we believe we are capable of attaining the level of shenren, and only if we learn to carry, deep in our heart, the pure jade of inner wisdom.

- Take the time to read each chapter, one at a time, and think and feel about how you can apply each particular passage and teaching to your life.

- There is no hurry, no time imposed by some outside source in which to do this.

- Take all the time you need to move deeply into this text.

- If you really spend the time to sit with each step, each commentary, each practice, you will know when it is time to move on to the next one.

- If you really allow yourself to go deeply into each passage, you will know which ones apply to you at any given moment.

- Take your time, move slowly, breathe deeply all the way from your heels.

---

1. Ellen M. Chen, *The Tao Te Ching: A New Translation with Commentary* (St. Paul, MN: Paragon House, 1989), 205.

66

Great rivers and seas can act as
the lord of a hundred river valleys.
This is because they flow downstream.
Therefore they can act as
the lord of a hundred valleys.
In this way, the sage who wishes
to be a guide to others
must place himself lower than them.
If he wants to lead the people
he must follow from behind.
Thus the sage dwells above the people
yet the people do not feel burdened.
He walks before them
yet the people are not harmed.
This is why all under Heaven supports him
without ever tiring of it.
Because he does not struggle with anyone
no one under Heaven struggles with him.

The Commentary

All rivers and streams run to the sea. This is why we think of the great rivers and oceans as being lords over the smaller rivers and streams.

The sage puts himself lower than the people around him if he wants to be a good influence over them. It is by being humble, by leading from behind, that he can have the most positive influence. He can be a leader and the people around him do not feel burdened. He puts himself forward but in such a way that his followers are not harmed. In this way, he is supported by the whole world, which, because of his humble and sincere ways, does not tire of doing so. Because he does not struggle or contend with anyone, no one struggles or contends with him.

Taoism teaches us that when we leak or expend chi uselessly, we suffer. This is the reason behind Taoist sexual yoga, such as semen retention. We can leak chi in other ways as well: by letting in violent or disturbing images from movies or television; by gaping at car accidents we pass by on the road; and by not paying attention to when we are overdoing or overextending ourselves toward others, toward work, toward trying to be "the best."

This is all counter to the Watercourse Way. To struggle is different from persisting. To persist means taking each step on our journey with fortitude and grace. It means keeping up our practices of meditation, tai chi, chi gong, *dao-in* (Taoist yoga), or study. It means keeping our perspective when things get rough.

THE PRACTICE Gathering Chi from the Earth and the Sun

Where are you struggling? Is this struggling necessary? Is it improving the situation? Most likely, the answers to these three questions will point you in a direction of where you are expending or "leaking" energy or chi in your life. The opposite of leaking energy is gathering it. Here is one way to do that:

- Stand with your feet flat upon the Earth, shoulder-width apart.

- Tuck your pelvis in slightly and keep your head and neck straight, as if being held by a thread from the bai hui point on the top of your head.

- Hold your hands in front of you, level with your lower dantian, palms facing down.

- Sink roots down deep into the Earth, reaching at least three times the length of your body.

- Move your arms out in a big circle as you bend your knees, sinking down toward the Earth.

- Gather yin chi up from the Earth.

- Bring your hands up, palms facing the Heavens, straight in front of you, all the way up to the third eye level.

- Then turn your palms down and guide the chi down through the central channel (chong mai) to your lower dantian.

- Do this nine times.

- Then stand as before.

- Swing your arms out to two sides in a bigger circle, gathering yang chi from the sun, the stars, and the Heavens.

- Bring your arms together over your head and guide the chi down your central channel once again, palms down, to your lower dantian.

- Do this nine times.

- Allow yourself to really feel the connection to the Earth from the bottoms of your feet (the yong chuen point) and to the sun and stars from the top of your head (the bai hui point).

- Feel the strong energy of the Earth and of the sun and stars come into your body as you gather from below and from above.

- Feel that strong energy moving down through the very center of your body, filling your dantian with healing chi.

- When you are finished, place your hands over your lower dantian and breathe into this center for at least nine deep breaths.

- Circle your palms slowly over your dantian, nine times in one direction and then nine times in the other.

- You will feel refreshed and renewed by this practice. You can do it any time your energy seems low or obstructed.

- Of course you can do it more than nine times, but that is a good starting place, because nine is made up of three threes and is considered to be a very auspicious number.

67

Everyone says that
my teaching of Tao is great.
It does not seem to resemble
anyone else's teaching.
It is because it is great
that it does not resemble
anyone else's teaching.
If it were like everyone else's teaching
it would have been useless.
I have three treasures.
I save them and keep them safe.
The first is compassion.
The second is simplicity.
The third is not wanting to be first.
Because I have compassion I can be brave.
Because I value simplicity I can be vast.
Because I do not care to be first
I can instead become ruler over all.
Today people abandon compassion
and only *act* bravely.
They abandon simplicity
and only act like they have it all.
They abandon placing themselves last
and instead place themselves first.
This way lies death.
If one uses compassion
then victory is assured
and defense will be long-lasting.
Heaven guards all things
with compassion.

The Commentary

Lao Tzu says his teaching is great—great in the sense of vast, unlimited. His teaching is not like anyone else's. This is also what makes it so great. If it were like anyone else's teaching, it would be worthless.

He then tells us about three priceless treasures that he possesses—compassion, simplicity, and not wanting to be first. Because of his compassion, he can also be brave. Being simple, he can be vast. And because he is not interested in being first in line, he can become a great leader.

Yet most people only *pretend* to be compassionate, and so they only *act* brave. By abandoning simplicity, people end up wanting too many material things. And by not wanting to be last in line, they always strive to become first in line.

This is wrong, says Lao Tzu; it leads to dissipation and death. It is by using the first of the Three Treasures, compassion, that we can become victorious in life. If we use compassion in our defense, our defense will always be strong. It is because of compassion that Heaven guides and protects us.

The second treasure is simplicity. This is one of the core teachings of Taoism: keep it simple. Complicated, whether in lifestyle or in spiritual teachings, is not necessarily better. Most chapters in the *Tao Te Ching* are simple. There is not a lot of flowery language or arcane hard-to-understand teaching. It helps to know a little about Chinese culture and history, but anyone can pick up the Old Boy's book and learn something to apply to their life right away.

The last treasure—not wanting to be first, not wanting to be at the head of the line, the top of the heap, the most visible and important person—is also very simple yet extremely powerful. This ties into the principle of pu or naturalness. It is in being our true, authentic natural self that we will find ourselves aligned with Tao. Things always change, the *I Ching* tells us. They change and transform, and so do we. It is when we try to call attention to ourselves in an egoic fashion that our downfall is sure to come.

At the end of the step, Lao Tzu returns to the first treasure, compassion. It is with compassion, he says, that Heaven guards all things. This kind of compassion, toward others as well as ourselves, is a sign of great strength. To serve others in a compassionate way is the way of the sage. Chuang Tzu says:

> To serve one's own heart-mind is to be free from both joy and sadness; to accept whatever is beyond your control, that is called true virtue. By doing what must be done, without thinking of one's self, you will not have time to worry about life and death. Just continue in this way and all will be well.[1]

The heart (xin) is seen as the ruler of the body or the sovereign of all the organs. It is also called the Crimson Palace (*jiang gong*). It is here that spiritual transformation happens.

The heart is not only the home of the shen or spiritual consciousness but also the seat of wisdom and spiritual growth. It is also the home of what we in the West call the mind or the intellectual mind. As such it has to do with cognitive function. An imbalance in the heart energy can cause disturbed or muddled thinking, short-term memory loss, insomnia, and hysteria.

Many of us have an overstimulated xin. We have a multitude of related and often unrelated thoughts going on in our head constantly. The heart is also associated with the fire element; it is the fire of uncontrolled thought processes that causes so much suffering for many of us.

In Taoist cosmology, there are two kinds of xin. One is the spirit of humans (*renxin*) and the other is the spirit of Tao (*taoxin*). Taoxin is also called Radiant Mind or Spirit (*zhaoxin*). This is the xin that we seek to connect with in our meditation practice and that needs to be nourished by our attitudes and practices in order for our spiritual nature to grow.

THE PRACTICE Slow Breathing

In sitting meditation, we seek to slow down the madly racing horse of our mind. One way to do that is to put our focus on our breath. This practice is a good way to slow our breathing and thereby slow the racing horse.

- Sit or lie down and begin breathing slowly and deeply.

- Feel your breath coming into your body, through your nose, and down into your lower dantian.

- Feel your breath leaving your body, up from your lower dantian, and then out through your nose or your mouth.

- After a few moments pause on each inhale and then on each exhale.

- Find the place of utter stillness between each breath.

- Breathe in, hold your breath for a count of three, and then exhale.

- At the end of your exhale, hold your breath again for a count of three.

- Find that deep place of utter stillness that happens between each breath.

- Let your mind drop down to the very bottom of your lower dantian.

- Feel the fire of your heart-mind move slowly down through the center of your body until it rests beneath the water of the lower dantian.

- Picture the crucible or cauldron of your lower dantian being fired up by this heart energy.

- Feel the transformation of the jing or generative energy being slowly refined and transformed into pure chi or vital energy.

- You may feel a sense of warmth or tingling in this area, or you may not.

- Feel your whole being slowly sinking down to the watery depths of your lower dantian.

- Allow your thoughts, your fears, and your questions to dissolve into the water, into smoke, into pure spirit.

- When you are finished, rub your hands together thirty-six times and then hold them over your eyes, breathing the warmth of your palms into your eyes.

- Then, with your palms still over your eyes, rotate your eyes nine times in one direction and then nine times in the other direction.

- To end, rub your face up and down, gently.

---

1. Solala Towler, *Chuang Tzu: The Inner Chapters* (London: Watkins Publishing, 2010), 77.

68

True warriors do not fight.
One who excels in battle
does not lose his temper.
One who is skillful at defeating his enemies
does not look for war.
Those who are good at leading others are humble.
This is called the *power of not contending.*
This is called *the strength to rule others.*
This is called *uniting with Heaven,*
the perfection of the ancients.

The Commentary

True martial artists are taught that, for the most part, it is best to avoid a fight. If they must fight, they should make sure it is over with as quickly as possible. They are also careful not to lose their temper and thus lose their center. If they can fight from their still center, they will be much more effective.

The highest level of warrior, Lao Tzu tells us, is the one who remains humble and does not go looking for a fight. Lao Tzu calls this the power of not contending. Notice that he uses the word *power* to describe the ability to avoid conflict. This is a power that comes only from one who has cultivated himself. This kind of warrior is not concerned with fighting but with avoiding fights. One must train to become a true warrior in order to gracefully avoid using a warrior's skills. This is called *Wen Wu Xing,* the Path of the Cultured Warrior.

The Cultured Warrior avoids fighting, yet has the inner strength to defend himself if he needs to. He has trained in certain techniques that allow him to vanquish an enemy or aggressor quickly and with the least amount of damage. It is interesting to note that in ancient times, martial artists also trained in the healing arts so they could take care of their opponent once the fight was over and their opponent was seriously injured.

This is also called the strength to rule others. The Cultured Warrior rules by his inner strength and not by the force of his personality. He inspires others so that they too can become Cultured Warriors. In this way he is uniting his spirit with all of life or "all under Heaven."

Becoming a Cultured Warrior takes training and practice, as well as the wisdom of how to apply it, yet it is something anyone can learn. With enough patience, with enough openness to learning and change, anyone can become this kind of warrior.

First, we must become masters of our own chi center, especially our lower dantian. If we are doing sword practice, we must learn to channel our chi from our lower dantian and up along our arm and into the sword itself and then send it out through the point of the sword. In this way, a sword or other weapon becomes an extension of our lifeforce. When we accomplish this, we will have mastered our own chi and our own spirit.

Of course we will probably not be wielding an actual sword, but the principle is the same. If we are strong in our chi center and can channel that energy in a way that is useful and powerful, we will be like the strong warriors of old.

Relaxation is the key. We must learn to not only relax the body but also relax the mind. Then we must learn to relax our chi, our internal energy. Once we can do that, our chi can travel freely throughout the body. But first we must learn how to build it up in our dantian, the field of elixir. Everyone has this field, but few people have developed it.

THE PRACTICE   The Warrior's Breath

What happens when we are frightened or have a shock? We often stop breathing or hold our breath. It is by training ourselves to breathe deeply and slowly, no matter what situation we find ourselves in, that we will be able to breathe as a warrior. This is called "the warrior's breath."

- Sit and begin to breathe, deeply and slowly, into your lower dantian.

- Feel your energy begin to focus and flow into this important center.

- Feel it as a point of power.

- Feel your strength and power sitting quietly in this center, ready to be called upon at a moment's notice.

- Feel it as a kind of stillness, a stillness that can transform to an explosive kind of power when needed.

- This practice will create the foundation that you will build upon in order to find your own inner warrior.

- Once you have perfected the warrior's breath, you need to learn how to relax your mind. Relaxing your mind frees up much of your chi.

- If your mind is relaxed your reflexes will be faster.

- You will be able to react to any danger—physical or emotional—and respond very quickly and with the least amount of stress.

- You must cultivate a calm and clear mind if you truly want to walk the path of the Cultured Warrior.

- This warrior's power should never be used to start a fight or to force one's will onto others.

- This kind of power is not for the conquest of others; rather it is for perfecting one's own inner spirit and for protecting the helpless and unfortunate.

69

In warfare there is a saying.
"I do not make the first move
  but act as guest.
I dare not advance one inch
  but will withdraw a foot."
This is called *advancing without moving,*
  or *rolling up the sleeves without bearing arms,*
  or *capturing the enemy without attacking.*
There is no greater misfortune than
  underestimating the enemy.
By underestimating the enemy I will lose.
When two armies are equally matched
  the compassionate one will win.

The Commentary

Once again we see Lao Tzu using the metaphor of war. For many people, life itself is like warfare. They are constantly at odds with other people, always strategizing about how to get ahead of others, always on the defensive.

Lao Tzu tells us that in overtures toward others, we can sometimes "disarm" them or place them at ease. By not being aggressive, by rolling up our emotional sleeves and showing others that we have no "weapons," we can often allow them to relax.

As in Step 67, we are taught to use compassion when dealing with others—those others who are so quick to feel threatened or slighted or attacked. By using compassion as a kind of strength, we can allow them to understand that they are not being threatened. It is by being strong in our own being and centered in our compassion that we can begin to offer some kind of healing to the people who are suffering so much in the world.

THE PRACTICE Gathering Chi from the Four Directions

This is a practice to strengthen our chi system. It helps us become strong and centered people, much like the one that Lao Tzu describes in this step.

- Begin by facing toward the east. This is the direction of the sunrise and represents new beginnings. It is associated with the Green Dragon, the liver, the color green, and the season of spring.

- Invoke the energy of this direction before you begin moving.

- Stand with your feet planted firmly on the Earth.

- Send your roots down into the Earth as far as at least three times the length of your body. (See Step 70.)

- Bring your hands up in front of your lower dantian, palms facing each other.

- In your mind's eye, see a ball of chi, about the size of a soccer ball, between your hands.

- Bring your palms together, then apart, and then together again, until you feel some sort of substance between your hands, a sensation of pressure in your palms.

- You can also alternate between inhaling when you bring your palms away from each other and exhaling as you bring them together.

- By gathering chi in this way you will fill your palms or lao gong points.

- Now bring your arms down to your sides, with palms facing up.

- Slowly raise your arms in front of you, all the way up to your bai hui point at the top of your head, palms facing down.

- Beam the chi from your palms into your bai hui, with your arms over your head, fingers pointing to each other.

- Lace your fingers together over your head and turn your palms up to the Heavens. Stretch your hands up as far as you can, giving your spine a good stretch.

- Stretch up three times. Then, with your fingers still laced together, slowly bend over until you can place your palms on the ground between your feet. (If you cannot bend that far, bend as far as you can and use your mind to send the chi from your palms into the Earth.)

- Bend a little more and touch the ground in front of your right foot and then your left.

- This time imagine that you are collecting yin energy from the Earth.

- Then straighten your body and stand with your arms down at your sides.

- Raise your arms again as before, holding the chi ball, all the way up to your bai hui point.

- Beam the Earth chi into your bai hui.

- Open your chest by spreading your elbows.

- Turn your palms down, fingertips pointing to each other. Slowly bring your hands all the way down to your waist, guiding the chi through your central channel (chong mai), which runs down through the center of your body, all the way down to your lower dantian.

- When your hands reach the level of your navel, turn your palms so that they face your abdomen; embrace the ball of chi in front of your lower dantian.

- After holding this position for a few moments, draw your hands in toward your abdomen. When they are an inch away from it, bring your hands along your sides and let them fall naturally.

- Do this same routine facing south, which is associated with the Red Phoenix, the heart, the direction of joy and expansion, the color red, and the season summer.

- Then do it again facing west, associated with the White Tiger, the lungs, the energy of gathering (bringing in the harvest), the color white, and the season autumn.

- Then do it one more time facing north, associated with the Black Turtle, the kidneys, the energy of "returning to the root," and the season winter.

- Keep an image of yourself inhabiting the center point of the circle as you turn toward each direction. This center is associated with the Yellow Dragon, the spleen, the energy of being grounded and rooted in the Earth, the color yellow, and the seasons of Indian summer or the time between each season.

70

My words are easy to understand and to practice
yet under Heaven no one understands them
or attempts to practice them.
My teachings have an ancient source.
My actions have their own master.
Most people do not understand my words
so they do not understand me.
Those who understand me are few,
those who follow me are even less.
This is why the sage dresses in coarse clothing
and holds precious jade in her heart.

The Commentary

Lao Tzu's teachings are indeed simple and easy to understand but difficult to put into practice. Many thousands if not millions of people have read his writings over the past twenty-five hundred years. However, most people who encounter the text may be inspired by a few of the chapters, but do not put them into serious practice. To truly understand Lao Tzu's teaching, it is not enough to just read them with the mind; we also need to read them with our hearts.

Chuang Tzu says:

> You must center your heart and mind in perfect
> harmony. Do not listen with your ears but with
> your heart. Do not listen with your heart but with
> your chi. Hearing stops with the ears, thoughts
> and ideas stop with the mind. Your chi or vital
> energy, though, resides in stillness and is open

and receptive to all things. True knowledge or Tao
resides in stillness and emptiness.[1]

As mentioned previously, Lao Tzu's teachings did not originate with
him but were the result of his long study and cultivation over many
years. Here he admits that his ideas are not only his but also those of
masters, who were already ancient in Lao Tzu's time.

He goes on to explain that actions or deeds also have their source in
Tao. If our actions or deeds are grounded in Tao, they will bear good
fruit. It is not enough just to be conversant with the ideas and philosophy of the *Tao Te Ching*; we must also study and apply all the practices
that are found within it. Not only that, we must take the time to study
Lao Tzu's work and really understand it, while remembering that each
time we read it, we will see something new. From one year to the next,
from one life to the next, his teachings will bring something fresh to
our understanding.

THE PRACTICE   In the Garden

Our journey is one of self-discovery and self-realization. It is a journey
of ever-growing awareness and a deepening of our heart. We cannot
just read the words in the *Tao Te Ching* and think that we have understood them. We must not just read them with our mind but also instill
them in our heart, like precious jewels. To really understand them, we
have to live them.

How can you do this?

- By paying attention, by reading the steps with intention,
  by applying them to every aspect of your existence.

- There is no part of your life to which Lao Tzu's
  guidance cannot be applied, whether it is your spiritual
  life, your emotional life, your psychological life, your

health issues, your financial issues, your family issues, your issues with society, or lastly, your issues with your own personal cultivation.

- You must grow this spiritual garden with care and attention.

- You must pay attention not only to the flower but also to the fruit.

- You must pay attention not only to the fruit but also to the stems.

- You must pay attention not only to the stems but also to the roots.

- And you must pay attention not only to the roots but also to the whole plant.

- To really understand the *Tao Te Ching* and be able to apply its teachings and practices will take time.

- This journey will be a long one, but it will also be full of surprises and adventures.

- It will not be finished quickly, perhaps not even in one lifetime.

- Yet it is the most important, most gratifying, most amazing and magical journey you can undertake.

---

1. Solala Towler, *Chuang Tzu: The Inner Chapters* (London: Watkins Publishing, 2010), 74.

71

To know that one does not know is best.
To not know yet think one knows
will lead to affliction (*bing*).
The sage is free from affliction
because he sees affliction as affliction
and so does not experience affliction.

The Commentary

To realize that we truly do not know anything is the first step on the road to knowledge. Conversely, to think we know something we don't sets us up for affliction. The word used in this step is *bing*, which can also be translated as "mental sickness."

This is an important point. It is through *thinking* that we understand that we have set ourselves up for affliction. To know that we do not know leads to the door of true understanding. It can be uncomfortable to admit we don't know everything, yet it is the mark of the sage to admit to not knowing *anything*.

It is also the mark of the sage to admit to faults and mistakes. In this way, what the world sees as affliction, the sage sees as opportunities for learning. In this way he is above the afflictions and thus does not experience them as such.

As mentioned in the previous step, the wisdom of Lao Tzu cannot help us unless we apply it to our lives. True wisdom is not found by just reading books—even this book. True wisdom comes from experience and practice.

THE PRACTICE Applying Your Knowledge

Of course, when we first encounter Tao, it is difficult to know how to apply these teachings to our lives. It is only over the course of time that we will bear the fruits of our cultivation practice. But here is a place to start.

- Think of three problems or challenges in your life.

- Now look at each one and consider how Lao Tzu's teachings of wu wei, Watercourse Way, and the value of the worthless can help you with them.

- See how you can approach these problems or challenges in a new way.

- Write them down and then write down the principle of Lao Tzu that may be helpful with each one.

- Of course, just writing them down will do you no good unless you then apply Lao Tzu's wisdom to your life.

- Trust that these teachings are valuable, priceless even.

- Try taking a different approach than the one you usually would.

- Try embodying the principle in your everyday life.

- You will be surprised by how easy it really is, and you will most probably be pleased with the results.

72

When people do not fear the power of the ruler,

they will bring about calamity.

If the ruler does not force himself into their home

and does not control their livelihood,

the people will not rebel against her.

This is why the sage knows herself

yet keeps herself hidden.

She respects herself

but does not make a show of herself.

She leaves that but takes this.

The Commentary

As in other steps, this one can be read as describing the way a government ought to rule, or it can be read as describing the inner state of the cultivator. We saw this in Step 63, in which we were given the advice of taking care of small problems before they became big ones. Here too we are given the advice of taking care of little fears or problems so that they do not come back as even larger ones.

We are also given the advice not to interfere with the lives of others. We should not force our way into their lives (home) or their way of life (livelihood). It is not up to us to criticize or condemn others for how they are living their lives. We should only offer advice and give it if we are asked for it.

Ho Shang Kung translates the third and fourth lines as, "This means that the heart serves as a dwelling of spirits. One ought to enlarge and not narrow it. Whereby man lives, this is by his possessing the spirits. The spirits rely on emptiness and enjoy stillness."[1]

Taoists believe in many natural spirits. These spirits are said to dwell all around us, even in our own body. Some of these spirits are guiding spirits, which are drawn to students of self-cultivation. The pureness of our practice draws them to us. These kinds of spirits also come from nature, from the sun, the moon, and the stars. Some of them may even come from other life forms, such as trees and animals. All so-called primitive peoples have learned ways to communicate with these kinds of spirits.

The second type of spirits may be thought of as ancestor spirits. These kinds of spirits come to us from our ancestral heritage.

The third kinds are body spirits. They are the spirits that came with us in our body when we incarnated into this world. They live in various organs and other parts of our body. They can also influence our mental, emotional, and spiritual health.

What Ho Shang Kung is talking about is working with our shen, our spiritual center, which resides in our heart center. If we can gather some of these spirits from various parts of our being into our heart center, we will greatly benefit. Master Xuezhi Hu says, "Disciplining one's heart is a very important principle for Tao-pursuing practitioners."[2] Of course, when he says "disciplining one's heart," it also means disciplining one's mind. In many cases, it is our overdeveloped yet little-understood mind that causes our problems in life. Surely there are limitations with living in a physical body, yet even those can be greatly affected, both positively and negatively, by our mind.

THE PRACTICE Working with the Spirits

Our mind-intent allows us to gather these three levels of spirits into our heart so that they can guide and protect us along our journey.

- Sit or lie down, close your eyes, and begin breathing into the lower dantian.

- After a few moments, bring your attention to your heart center.

- Open your mind to receiving guidance from your indwelling spirits.

- As mentioned, some of them are your ancestors. These may be your spiritual ancestors, not just your genetic relatives. They may even be from a very different country or culture than your forebears.

- Others are comprised of various body spirits, which reside in your various organ systems or even in other areas of your body.

- In later Taoist practices, there were different meditations that viewed these body spirits as various gods and goddesses.

- These gods and goddesses were viewed through inner journeying and could have a positive affect on the meditator's whole system.

- Gather these spirits into your heart, filling your heart center with light and healing energy.

- Feel the energy of these tiny spirits filling your heart-mind.

- This is not just an exercise in using your imagination.

- These spirits are real.

- You may also see them as spiritual entities.

- They are there to support your life.

- Feel these helpful guiding spirits as they link up in your heart center.

- You may feel a physical sensation, or you may feel nothing at all.

- You may visualize this gathering of spirits as colors or some other kind of symbol, such as an angelic presence or even Kuan Yin (Guan Yin), the goddess of compassion.

- Or you may see nothing at all.

- Know that whatever you sense, even if they seem to be visitations by beings from another place, these are projections of your own precious spiritual energy.

- The helping spirits may take the form of other spiritual beings in order to communicate with you.

- Enjoy them, attend to them, take in their guidance, and then, when you are finished with the meditation, gently let all the spirits go back to their former dwelling places inside your body or back to nature.

- If you have received guidance or healing at this time, give thanks to all of your helping spirits—from nature, from your spiritual ancestors, or from your own energy system.

---

1. Eduard Erkes, *Ho-Shang-Kung's Commentary on Lao-Tse* (Zurich: Artibus Asiae Publishers, 1950), 122.
2. Xuezhi Hu, *Revealing the Tao Te Ching* (Los Angeles: Ageless Classics Press, 1995), 202.

73

Those who are brave but impetuous will be killed.

Those who are brave but not impetuous will live.

Of these two,

one brings benefit and one brings harm.

Who knows why Heaven dislikes the first.

Even the sage does not understand this.

The Tao of Heaven does not contend

yet always remains victorious.

It does not use words

yet is always responsive.

It does not force anything

yet everything goes its way.

It is always calm yet ever resourceful.

The net of Heaven is vast.

Its web is wide yet nothing slips through.

The Commentary

People who are brave but impetuous or who lack self-control will be defeated, while those who are brave yet have self-control will not be. This also refers to the person who is practicing self-cultivation and works to align himself with Tao and the one who does not.

Words cannot be used to describe Tao, yet it is always responsive to the clear heart and the calm mind. It does not force anything, and so everything goes along naturally and harmoniously. Its energy can be described as calm and serene and infinitely resourceful. The reality of Tao is a vast net with a wide web—nothing escapes it.

We see in this step that just being brave is not enough. We need to have self-control as well. If we want to travel the road of Tao, the road of life, we need to be brave enough to use nonaction in our every action.

It takes great courage to walk this path. It is not for everyone. It is not for those who like to follow orders and want to join an organization or religious cult where they will be told what to do, what to eat, what to wear, or what to believe.

This kind of road is created anew with each step. It requires us to be brave in our journey toward oneness, to be discerning in our choices, to be faithful to our quest for self-knowledge and self-growth. It requires us to keep our eyes and heart-mind wide open, our senses alive to each unfolding moment, our intentions fully and deeply engaged.

The Tao of Heaven does not use words to communicate, yet its message is always clear: Go slowly, be humble, take the Watercourse Way, be simple, be natural, and be open. It does not force anything to happen, yet everything unfolds just as it should be. Wouldn't it be great if our lives unfolded in just this way?

They can if we are true to our quest, if we keep the lines of communication open between our higher and lower self, if we stay on course, and if we forget about being first but are happy to be last.

THE PRACTICE   Swallowing the Sun and Moon

How do we do all this? Connecting our small nature with the big nature outside of us helps. Here is a simple exercise.

- Stand facing the sun in the morning.

- Close your eyes and inhale—"swallow" the light of the sun at least nine times, though thirty-six times is even better. You can do this by imagining you are swallowing or by actively swallowing.

- Bring the light of the sun all the way down into your lower dantian.

- Fill your elixir field with this energizing, yang energy.

- The sun does not have to be shining for this practice to work. Just face the sun, even if it is behind the clouds, and see its light shining with your inner vision.

- Another way to do this practice is to "swallow" the moon, nine to thirty-six times.

- Again, you do not have to actually see the moon for this practice to work.

- Even if it is behind clouds or mist, you can still see the cooling energy of the moon filling your lower dantian with calming, yin energy.

- You can also use this exercise if you feel that your yin energy needs a boost or if you feel your yang energy is too strong and you wish to balance it with some yin energy.

- This may seem very fanciful and "unreal," but remember that both the sun and the moon greatly affect every living thing on the Earth, including you.

- By consciously bringing this sun and moon energy into your being, you greatly enhance their affect on you.

74

When people do not fear death
how can the threat of death scare them?
If the ruler makes sure that
people do fear death
and when one of them breaks the law
and he executes them,
who will dare to break the law?
There is always an executioner ready.
But if you try to take the place of the executioner
it will be like taking the place of a master carver.
If you try to take the place of a master carver
it will be very difficult to avoid injuring yourself.

The Commentary

Once again we see the analogy or metaphor of the powerful ruler who threatens his people with death if they break the law. If these people do not fear death, how can he have power over them? Yet this ruler insists on executing those who disobey the law. He always has an executioner ready.

Of course, this can also be read as meaning when we have no fear of death, death does not have a hold on us. If our spirit is strong and our mind is clear, no one can exert control over us. If we go against Tao, against the flow of life, there will be consequences. The "executioner" is none other than the law of karma or the law of cause and effect. This is a law that none of us can escape. Yet we often assume the role of executioner of our own lives. We hold the threat of punishment over ourselves until we are too scared to act at all, for fear of retribution from on high.

If we try to take up the role of the master carver when we are not properly trained as one, there is a great likelihood that we will end up injuring ourselves with the chisels and hammers.

Whatever we are afraid of has a hold on us. If we had no fear of being punished—by God, by our parents, by society, by ourselves—wouldn't life be much sweeter?

A universal response network exists across all time and space. Whatever kind of energy we put out will give us a like response. If we put out nothing but negativity and fear, we will receive nothing but negativity and fear in response. If we put out joy and positive energy, we will, in turn, receive the same.

Usually the energy we put out is a mixture of both positive and negative. Most people are not even aware of what kind of message they are sending. Therefore, it helps to have a teacher or a loving partner to point this out to us. We must be humble and brave enough to acknowledge our faults or mistakes.

It takes a long time to become a sage. It takes a long time to just become a good student. Patience is one of the best tools we can possess. Patience and a sense of humor are essential on this journey of ours, as is the courage to be seen as thickheaded or clumsy, as in Step 20.

THE PRACTICE Taking Up the Tools of the Master

It is important not to claim to have abilities or knowledge that we do not truly possess. This is like setting ourselves up as a master carver when we don't really know how to use the tools. We will inevitably be injured.

So how do you know when you are ready to take up the tools of the master?

- You will receive signs from those around you, as well as from your own inner spirits.

- If you are aware of your inner spirits and they are gathered in good order, you will be able to receive messages and guidance from them.

- If they are instead scattered, this line of communication will be blocked.

- You must "keep the faith" that you are on the right path at the right time in the right way.

- "Faith" in Taoist practice means that you invest yourself totally in your practice.

- There is an old saying in China: "Although the rain waters broadly, it cannot save the plant that has no root. Although the gate of Buddhism is widely open, Buddha cannot help a person who refuses to enter."

- This also refers to the net of Tao.

- Though its mesh is wide, if you are not sincerely practicing, you will not be able to move through it.

- You must also be persistent in your practice.

- Persistence is like the river that flows down to the ocean yet does not run backward.

- This is also called the "indomitable spirit."

- This also means being flexible and not rigid, firm and determined, just and upright.

- For the high-level practitioner, another crucial principle is that of *wu* or comprehension or the power of understanding.

- It is not enough to blindly follow your teacher and do the movements, internal or external, by rote.

- You must take the time to really understand both the principles of Tao and their application in your life.

- This is true understanding.

75

People go hungry when the ruler
takes too much in taxes.
This is why the people are hungry.
People are difficult to govern
because the ruler interferes too much.
This is why the people are hard to govern.
People take death lightly
because the ruler demands too much of their life.
This is why people take death so lightly.
Only the ones who practice doing nothing (wu wei)
are able to value their life.

The Commentary

If the ruler takes too much in taxes, there is nothing left to buy food, and the people go hungry. If the ruler interferes too much in their lives, people are desperate and hard to govern. If the ruler makes too many demands on them, people no longer have the will to live.

This can also be read as not taking care of both our physical body and our spiritual body. By "taxing" our body, we exhaust ourselves. If we "interfere" with our physical body, our emotional body suffers. When our chi is too low, we cannot think clearly. When we exhaust ourselves physically, our emotions also suffer. What is a mild challenge when we're in balance can seem insurmountable when our chi is too low.

Also, if too many demands are put upon us by our job, our relationship, or our family, we will not value our life the way we do when things are going well. This is why it is so important to practice chi gong and stillness meditation. By doing these kinds of practices, we will have the tools to deal with difficult or challenging times.

As always, Lao Tzu recommends living our life from the place of wu wei. In this way, we will be able to value and enjoy all aspects of our life, from the easy to the challenging.

One of my teachers says he can describe the Taoist lifestyle in three words: "Take it easy!" Of course this doesn't mean being lazy or useless. It means: don't be too hard on yourself, don't take yourself too seriously, and don't make things more difficult than they have to be.

Sometimes we may think that to be "spiritual" means to be serious and sober at all times. After all, spirituality is a serious business, or so we think. But when we take ourselves too seriously, we lose all the joy and enjoyment of being on the path.

The journey we are on is one of joy and acceptance, of creativity and openness to change, of magic and miracles. It should be a dance, not a trudge. It should make us happy and not somber. It should introduce us to new wonders and amazing sights. It should take us to places we have never been before, or perhaps never even imagined.

This journey is just one step in front of the other. There is no special speed at which we need to travel—each one of us moves at his or her own pace. We cannot compare ourselves to anyone else. We are each on our own unique journey.

THE PRACTICE Walking Meditation

Speaking of stepping, here is a walking exercise from the Taoist tradition. Try this practice the next time you take a hike or are just walking across a parking lot.

- Begin by walking, paying special attention as you put one foot in front of the other.

- Move slowly but not too slowly.

- Be conscious of your feet connecting to the Earth and of your weight when it moves from one foot to the other as you put pressure on the ball of our foot, your yong chuen (kidney 1) point.

- By putting pressure here, you stimulate your kidney channel and thereby your kidney/adrenal organs.

- Fold your thumbs in toward the center of your hands, and close your fingers loosely around them.

- Keep your head up and drink in your surroundings. (This is just good general advice about everything in life.)

- Be conscious of your weight shifting from side to side, of connecting with the Earth with each step.

- Swing your arms naturally by your side, but not too vigorously. It is all a matter of balance. This is another great way to describe the Taoist lifestyle—it's all a matter of balance!

76

When we are born we are supple and tender
like a young plant.
When we die we become rigid and unyielding.
The ten thousand beings,
including plants and grasses,
when young are soft and pliable.
At their death they are dry and brittle.
Therefore we say that the stiff and unyielding
are the companions of death.
The soft and yielding are the followers of life.
In this way, an army may be strong
but it will be defeated.
A mighty tree may be strong
yet its branches may be broken off.
The hard and unyielding will fall
while the soft and yielding will overcome.

The Commentary

This is one of the most important steps in the whole book. If we learn how to apply the ideas in this one step, our whole life could change.

When we are young, we are soft and pliable, like a green plant. When our mind is malleable and not yet formed, we are open to new things. In the first years of our life, we must learn to speak whatever language our parents speak. We must learn how to crawl and then walk. We must learn how to eat. We must learn to differentiate ourselves from our surroundings. We must learn what it is to be human.

Not all of what we learn is good for us. We also learn how to lie, how to hide, how to throw a fit if we do not get what we want. We learn about sickness, about pain. Yet we also learn about love and joy and how lovely it is to share. We are on a grand adventure, learning all the ways there are in the world to grow. We learn how to give and how to celebrate. We learn how to laugh and to dance.

Then, as the years go by, our body, which we have often taken for granted in our youth and not always treated with the greatest respect, begins to age and to suddenly be full of aches and pains and even disease. We become set in our ways, no longer interested in new adventure. We become stiff, and we find ourselves complaining all the time.

Our interest in the world shrinks, as do our horizons. We become fearful and worrisome. And then, when our bodies are worn out or become diseased, we die.

Sometimes we die before our physical body does. We die because we have become so stiff and unyielding that our sense of adventure and fun and excitement has dwindled down to almost nothing. Yet, if we can keep a sense of childlike adventure and interest and excitement about life and all that we are learning and doing, perhaps we will not die before our time. Or, when our time does come, perhaps we will be ready and able to leave this plane of existence with no regrets and no sense of disappointment about our life. This would be aligning ourselves with the soft and yielding, what Lao Tzu calls "the followers of life."

We may spend a lot of time building what we think of as solid walls between ourselves and others, but like a mighty tree, our branches, once dried, can be easily broken off. However, if we are able to remain soft and yielding, like a young plant, we would be able to live our life with a sense of grace and gratitude, of joy and fulfillment, of bending but not breaking when confronted with adversity.

How can we remain like the young plant that Lao Tzu extols? We can begin by not abusing our body and spirit through bad diet and lifestyle choices. We can instead nurture our whole selves with good physical and spiritual nutrition. We can practice yoga, dao-in, tai chi, or chi gong. Each practice can help our body to remain flexible and strong. We can sit less and move more. We can learn to dance or else just free our spirit to move in whatever way we feel. We can engage in healthy sexual practices that do not deplete our energy.

Most important, we can let our minds remain open and interested, alert and attuned to what is going on around and within us. We can be open to new people, new places, new foods, new ideas, new thoughts, and new experiences. Then, even if our bodies begin to age or become injured or diseased, we will suffer less.

THE PRACTICE   Staying Young Chi Gong

Here are a few chi gong exercises to keep you young:

Embracing the Sun and the Moon

- Stand on the Earth and send your roots down, at least three times the length of your body.

- Move your arms in a big circle, as if you were embracing the moon.

- Bring that good yin energy of the moon into your whole body.

- Feel it fill you up with good energy.

- Then circle your arms again in an even bigger circle, embracing the sun.

- Bring all that strong yang energy of the sun into your body.

- You can do each circle three times or nine times or even thirty-six times.

- You can also do this small practice facing each of the four directions, starting with east, then south, then west, and then north.

- When you have finished, bring your palms together over your lower dantian and breathe deeply into this important energy center nine times.

- Finally, circle your palms over your abdomen—nine times in one direction and nine times in the other.

Spiraling Dragon

This next exercise, called Spiraling Dragon or Dragon Dance, comes from the ancient practice of dao-in. It is a good way to loosen up your spine and waist.

- Sit comfortably on a cushion or on the ground.

- Bring your hands together over your head, palms touching each other.

- Push your waist out to the right, pushing your elbows out to the right at the same time.

- Then push your waist and elbows out to the left.

- Do this at least nine to thirty-six times on each side.

- You can lower your arms as you do so, but always keep your palms together.

- Your spine will undulate like a snake as you do so.

- You can also pick up your speed as you go along.

- To close, bring your palms together in front of your middle dantian and breathe slowly for nine breaths.

- This exercise will open up your spine as well as your du mai channel, which runs up your spine and is one of the most important energy channels in your body.

Is the Way of Heaven not like stretching a bow?

What is too high must be lowered

and what is low must be raised.

What is too tight must be loosened

and what is too loose must be tightened.

The Way of Heaven

is to decrease the excessive

and add to the insufficient.

The way of humankind is not this way.

It detracts from those who have less

and gives to those who have too much.

Who has more than enough

and is willing to share it with the world?

Only those who have Tao.

The sage acts but does not seek credit.

She accomplishes much

but does not dwell on it.

She does not show off her virtue.

The Commentary

The Way of Heaven or Tao is like stretching a bow. Lao Tzu is speaking about the self-regulating aspect of Tao here. Tao regulates itself naturally, easily, much like the tightening or loosening of a bow. It always seeks balance. What is excessive, it decreases; what is insufficient, it increases.

Yet we are not like that. Society often takes away from those who have little and gives more to those who have much. We see this very clearly in our modern economic world, where the top one percent have most of the money and the power. Of course this has been going on for a long time, even in Lao Tzu's day.

Who is willing to share what they have and not live life from a position of fear of scarcity? Only those who are spiritually evolved, those men and women of Tao who are not afraid of sharing what they have, what they know, and what they have experienced with others. These kinds of people do good acts but don't make a big deal about it. They accomplish great things in the world but don't take credit for them. They do not make a show of their virtue or their spiritual attainments. These kinds of people, who are in short supply today, were in short supply even twenty-five hundred years ago.

Sometimes we may feel stretched like a bow. Our emotions, our physical energy, our mental processes—all of these can feel overextended and tight. One way to alleviate this is to study what is taught in any Taoist temple in China by tea masters. These are people who have perfected the art of *Cha Tao,* the Way of Tea. The Way of Tea involves slowing down and paying attention to the details—a cup of tea, an interaction with another person, a walk down or up the mountain, a tai chi or chi gong practice, and much else. As I wrote in my book *Cha Dao: The Way of Tea,* this is a path of introspection, meditation, and deep harmony with the Earth and living plants as a means to communicate with the spirit of both tea and Tao.

One of the ways tea masters practice is with the gongfu tea ceremony. In this ceremony, we use tiny little cups and a tiny little teapot, both of which are usually made of a special clay called *yixing,* which has been used for tea implements for hundreds of years. There is also a fair bit of "water play" involved, so we use a special tea table, which has either a tray built under it or a tube going down to a bowl under the table to catch the runoff that happens in the ceremony.

The experience we take with us from Taoist tea ceremonies can enhance our meditation practice and our general peace of mind. There are also many health benefits from drinking tea. Many teas contain large amounts of vitamin C and various minerals and are full of antioxidants.

Both green tea and *puer* (fermented) tea also contain a lot less caffeine than coffee or black tea.

Living our life with the Way of Tea allows us to slow down and pay attention to whatever experience is presenting itself in any given moment. We also learn to take the time to understand and respond harmoniously with it. It gives us permission to experience our life from the viewpoint of a student of the Way of Tea, the Watercourse Way.

THE PRACTICE   The Way of Tea

Of course we don't have to be masters at serving tea to enjoy sharing it with family or friends. As with most Taoist practices, there are some simple rules or steps involved. The first is to start with some good-quality tea. Since the ceremony uses a small amount of tea, investing in good-quality tea is well worth it.

There are many kinds of tea; experiment with different ones to see what you like best. Often puer tea is used in gongfu tea ceremony. This dark, earthy-tasting, fermented tea usually comes in hard bricks. To practice the way of tea:

- Use the special tea table with a tray underneath to catch water.

- Begin by heating water to just before boiling, or let it boil and then cool off a bit.

- While waiting for the water to boil, sit in quiet meditation or reflection.

- This will allow you to arrive gently into the present moment, the infinite moment of Tao.

- Start by pouring some hot water over the teapot and cups.

- Then, after pouring out the water, pour some tea leaves into the teapot and, after placing the lid on it, pour some more hot water over the pot.

- Remove the lid and pour water into the pot.

- Pour out the first infusion of tea in just a few moments. This is called "washing the leaves" and gets rid of any dust on the leaves.

- I also call this "waking up the leaves," which is especially helpful with puer tea, since the leaves are so tightly packed.

- After that, pour a new infusion and share it with others in the tiny teacups.

- Usually with the first cup, there is a little bit of ritual. For instance, you can hold the teacup between your thumb and index finger, with your third finger supporting it from below.

- Hold the cup in front of your chest in order to connect the *cha chi*, or chi of the tea, with your heart center for a few moments.

- Then look at the tea and enjoy its color. (I often use clear glass cups just for this purpose.)

- Smell the tea, allowing the fragrance to enter your body through your nose.

- Inhale the qualities of the tea in this way so that the cha chi enters you deeply.

- Then take three small sips of tea—the first with the tip of your tongue, the second with the middle of your tongue, and the third with the back of your tongue.

- You will notice a different flavor with each sip.

- After that, things get very relaxed; just enjoy drinking the tea, alone or with others.

- The Chinese tea ceremony is much more relaxed and informal than the Japanese tea ceremony.

- It is a time to share stories and perhaps some poetry and generally enjoy each other's company.

- Or you can sit together and enjoy the tea in silence. (You will be amazed at how much you can communicate by sitting in silence.)

- You will also be amazed at how many infusions you will be able to get out of a good-quality tea.

- This kind of practice is good for calming the heart-mind and for opening the senses, especially smell, taste, and even touch as you handle the earthenware cups and teapot.

step

78

Under Heaven there is nothing more yielding
and soft than water.
Yet for attacking what is hard and stiff
there is nothing better.
In this way, the weak can vanquish the strong
and the soft can overcome the hard.
Under Heaven, there is no one who does not know this,
yet no one practices it.
Therefore, the sage says,
the one who wishes to become a true lord
must suffer dishonor and disgrace.
The one who shares in the suffering of his country
deserves to be called Lord of All Under Heaven.
This is true yet sounds paradoxical.

The Commentary

In this step we have more description of the Watercourse Way. Even though water itself is soft and yielding, it has great power and strength. It is a good example of the virtue of being soft and yielding ourselves. People usually think of these attributes as weak or ineffectual, yet there is a force in them that will last much longer than aggressive and over-powering energy. Everyone knows this, says Lao Tzu, but very few put it into practice.

Ho Shang Kung says, "Water is able to annihilate fire. Yin is able to dissolve Yang. The tongue is weak, the teeth are strong, but the teeth perish before the tongue."[1]

In order to be a high-level master, we must be willing to experience the negative aspects of life. If we do not know what it is like to suffer as those around us suffer, then we will never be a good leader or teacher. This may sound strange, but it is true.

This way of the Watercourse Way is a fundamental teaching in Taoism. Water has the ability to flow downhill, to overcome obstacles, to adapt to any shape contained—these are also all attributes of the sage.

Lao Tzu goes even further to say that the "true lord" or sage must experience dishonor and disgrace. The one who shares the suffering of his people can be called a good ruler. Of course we can also understand this as becoming a "good ruler" of our own personal country.

How can we become a good ruler? By following the Watercourse Way, by being flexible and constant, by being humble and persistent, by being open and present. By honoring our blemishes and our imperfections. By becoming "one with loss." By suffering dishonor and disgrace with a graceful and accepting spirit. By overcoming the hard with the soft. By yielding or using the strength of the yin, the valley spirit, the mysterious feminine.

THE PRACTICE Spontaneous Chi Gong

To many people, the Watercourse Way sounds paradoxical and even strange. Yet followers of Tao have been working with these practices and concepts for thousands of years. Here is a way to connect with the yielding and the fluid:

- Stand with your feet flat on the Earth, roots heading downward, top of the head open to Heaven.

- Feel your water nature as you begin to slowly move in graceful waves.

- Don't think about how you are moving, just move.

- Let the chi of your body move you. Let your mind get out of the way, and let the inborn intelligence of your body show you how.

- This is called "spontaneous chi gong" and can be a place of deep healing.

- If you are playing music, let it be slow, sensual, and without words. Just let the music be the inspiration for your movement.

- Of course, you don't need music. Your own inner music will play for you once you have relaxed and gotten your Earthly mind out of the way.

- You may experience emotional release at this time—laughing or crying.

- Don't worry about it; just let it go.

- If it gets to be too much or too overwhelming, you can stop it by telling yourself to stop.

- Your movements may be small or they may be big.

- You may move very slowly or you may move quickly.

- You may move very gracefully or you may jerk around.

- As long as it is not your mind that is telling you how to move, it is fine.

- Let the spirit and the chi tell your body how to move.

- When you feel finished or if you feel tired or out of control just tell your mind to stop the movements.

- Stand for a few moments in stillness and peace, breathing into your lower dantian. Don't worry if you don't feel you have achieved anything by this exercise.

- Your mind will not necessarily understand what the chi of your body is doing at this time. Just relax and enjoy it.

---

1. Eduard Erkes, *Ho-Shang-Kung's Commentary on Lao-Tse* (Zurich: Artibus Asiae Publishers, 1950), 130.

79

After a quarrel some resentment remains.
How can this be good?
This is why the sage keeps his side of the contract
but does not demand anything of the other.
Virtuous people do not
concern themselves with contracts.
Those who are not virtuous make sure
to receive their end of the deal.
Although the Tao of Heaven has no partiality
it always supports the one of virtue.

The Commentary

After a quarrel between two people or even two nations, some uncomfortable feelings remain. How can this be good? This is why the sage does not always need to be right. He does not need to be the winner in every contest. Ordinary people always want to come out on top. But to the follower of Tao, there is no need to be "right" at all times.

Chuang Tzu says, "Allow distinctions to harmonize of their own accord, leaving different viewpoints as they are. Instead, dwell in the boundless and limitless. In this way we may be able to live out our years in peace."[1]

How can we give ourselves the great gift of not having to be "right" in every circumstance? This need to be right comes from fear, which comes from the dualistic mind or ego. We are so afraid that if we admit to being wrong, we will lose something, we will give something up. By giving in to someone else, we fear we will lose something of ourselves.

Yet if we are courageous enough, if we are humble enough, if we are strong enough, we can admit that our ideas of "right and wrong" are often based on false assumptions. Taoism teaches us that we need to go beyond limited concepts of "right and wrong." This can only come about when we seek out the light of true understanding,

THE PRACTICE   Giving Up the Need to Be Right

This step of giving up the need to be right is a big one. For many people, it may even be impossible. But for the traveler of Tao, it is crucial. If we do not take this important step, our way will not be clear, our journey will be fraught with confusion and doubt, and we may easily be lost in a sea of despair.

How can you let go of the need to be right?

- By breathing, by centering, by grounding, by balancing, by being in harmony with the world around you.

- By giving yourself some slack to be wrong.

- By not being afraid of being wrong.

- By learning from your "mistakes" and by using each interaction with others to practice "true understanding."

- Meditation helps, relaxation helps, following the flow of the Watercourse Way helps, surrendering to each unending moment helps, being humble and simple and natural helps, dancing tai chi or chi gong helps, reading the great masters helps, and applying what you read to what you do in life helps.

- This center point of Tao—between wrong and right—is what Lao Tzu has been sharing all along.

- By reading his words and applying them to your life, you will—with time, patience, and perseverance—become the kind of person who dwells in the boundless and limitless and who lives out your years in peace.

> If you look for your shen (spirit),
> it disappears.
> If you practice being yourself,
> it unites with you!
> It is such a simple reality,
> but takes a fool
> a million years to be enlightened.[2]

1. Solala Towler, *Chuang Tzu: The Inner Chapters* (London: Watkins Publishing, 2010), 72.
2. Hua-Ching Ni, *Mystical Universal Mother* (Santa Monica, CA: SevenStar Communications, 1991), 165.

80

A small country has few people.

It has soldiers but chooses not to use them.

Its people value their lives

and have no desire to travel far away.

Though there are boats and carts,

no one uses them.

Though there are weapons and armor,

no one displays them.

People have gone back to tying knots

and using them as writing.

They enjoy their food

and their clothing is beautiful.

They are at peace in their homes.

They find joy in their everyday life.

Nearby villages can see each other;

their dogs and chickens can be heard by each other.

Yet the people grow old and die

without seeking each other out.

The Commentary

Here we have a lovely description of the ideal kind of life, according to ancient Taoist principles. The population is small. While it does have soldiers, it does not use them. They have weapons of war, but choose not to display them. The people of this country enjoy their life so much that they do not feel the need to travel to other places. There are modes of transportation available, yet people do not use them, perhaps instead relying on their own two feet.

Instead of fancy methods of counting, they have gone back to using knotted string as a way of communicating. They eat well, with good natural food. They dress well, but simply.

They are at peace in their homes and find joy in their everyday lives. Other villages are near them, and they can hear the sounds of each other's animals, yet they feel no need to visit them. Instead they grow old gracefully and die well.

This is, of course, a metaphor for living a life in tune with the Way. The numbers of people who actually follow Lao Tzu's teaching have always been small. Of the many thousands of people who have read and even studied his work, very few of them put it into practice in their own lives. The ones who do live a life of simplicity and grace, of happiness and inner knowing.

It is not necessary to travel across the world to China to learn Taoist philosophy and practices. After all, Tao in the West is the same Tao as it is in the East. Our bodies and energy systems are the same as those of the ancient masters. Of course, our world is much more complicated and fragmented than theirs was. Our modern society has sped up immensely, and our ability to focus on the simple and slow has been much compromised. With the advent of social networking, many people are losing the ability to spend real time with others.

We don't need to turn back time to be able to work with Lao Tzu's ideas and practices. We can begin wherever we are, in whatever shape we are in, at any time of life.

While we don't actually have to go back to knotted string to communicate, we can still spend less time online and more real time with our friends and family. The Internet is a wonderful thing and has helped many of us who are doing research, keeping in touch with old friends, and making new ones around the planet, but if we only communicate online, we will find ourselves offline with the world around us.

If we do not take the time to study, digest, and go as deep as we can, we will never receive the benefits of our practice. If we try to learn too much too fast, our foundation will become weak. When storms of life batter our walls, the edifice of our life will crumble and fall.

Seeking good teachers is important. Practicing what they teach, even more so. The simpler our lifestyle is, the easier it will be to maintain. When we enjoy simple, natural food, our chi is stronger and better regulated. We can then maintain peace in our home, in our hearts, and in our minds. It becomes much easier to appreciate and enjoy our everyday life.

In this step, the description of a small village in which people live simple, full lives and do not contend with their neighbors is a beautiful image. While it would be impossible for everyone on this crowded planet of ours to live in small villages, we *can* live a life of inner simplicity and calmness, of peace and inner prosperity, of gratitude and grace, no matter where we are.

Chuang Tzu describes this kind of person like this:

> One who wishes to balance Heaven and Earth; who
> embraces the ten thousand beings; regards his body as a
> temporary dwelling; regards his senses as merely fleeting
> images; unifies his knowledge, and who doesn't experience
> death. Later, at a time of his choosing, he will leave the
> world of dust and return to the source of all life.[1]

Can we, in our postmodern age, be like these sages of whom Lao Tzu and Chuang Tzu speak? Can we live a life of "free and easy wandering"? Can we return to simplicity and naturalness and still live in an overly complicated and very unnatural world? Can we become as the ancient teachers, those who mastered the art of life and flew on the backs of dragons? Hua-Ching Ni says,

> Spiritual achievement, when described in a book, is
> like a picture of a dragon, a powerful spiritual creature
> colorfully drawn on paper. But one day, when your

energy is refined to the level of a high being, it is as if you transform yourself into a true dragon.[2]

THE PRACTICE   Taoist Advice for Modern Times

Lao Tzu lived in a much simpler society and time than we do, yet he was already concerned with how complicated and empty and violent the world around him was. There is still hope that we, as travelers of the inner landscape, will be able to find our way out of the brambles and the thickets of a world lost in greed and hate and find ourselves at the end of our journey, stronger and more clear, more balanced and more joyful than we started out. Our time is so much more complicated and empty and violent than Lao Tzu's, yet he has provided us with the pathway out of the thicket:

- It is all a matter of balance, says Lao Tzu, of balance and paying attention to the small things—like being at peace in your home and enjoying your everyday life.

- It is in learning the lessons of nonstriving and not doing, speaking without using words, and being satisfied with what *is* happening instead of what you *want* to happen.

- It is in learning how you listen to your inner guide and how to breathe deeply, with your whole body and being.

- It is in learning to trust and to access the lifeforce of the universe, of being at one with the world around you, and being satisfied with what you have, what you are, what you know.

---

1. Solala Tower, *Chuang Tzu: The Inner Chapters* (London: Watkins Publishing, 2010), 99.
2. Hua-Ching Ni, *Enlightenment: Mother of Spiritual Independence* (Santa Monica, CA: SevenStar Communications, 1989), 165.

81

Truthful words are not necessarily beautiful.

Beautiful words are not necessarily true.

Sages do not argue.

Those who argue are not sages.

Those who have true knowledge

are different from those with book knowledge.

Those who have book knowledge are not wise.

The sage does not accumulate possessions.

Because he acts for others he has more for himself.

The more he gives to others

the more he gains for himself.

Tao benefits all and does no harm.

The person of Tao acts but does not contend;

he is in harmony with all under Heaven.

The Commentary

Step 81 is the culmination of the book. The truth does not always come in attractive packages, says Lao Tzu. Truthful words are not necessarily beautiful. Likewise, beautiful words are not always truthful.

As Chuang Tzu reminds us, "Tao is hidden behind partial understanding, and the meaning of our words is hidden behind a screen of flowery rhetoric."[1] It is all too easy to hide behind this screen of flowery rhetoric and speak but not say anything of real value. There are too many glib teachers who know how to "talk the talk" without revealing much of the actual truth. The sage or the true spiritual teacher, on the other hand, does not need so many words to point to the truth. This kind of teacher knows how to teach without using words. Their teachings are expressed through their very being.

This kind of teacher does not argue abstract religious or spiritual points. True knowledge is not found only in books, nor is true understanding reached only with the mind. It is felt and experienced in the belly, in the dantian, our "field of elixir." True wisdom is not found only in intellectual pursuits but also in the small everyday interactions with the world around us.

When we first embark on our journey, we may read holy books describing the lives of enlightened beings. These books can be very inspirational, but when we have reached some level of spiritual achievement, they become descriptions of our own life.

It is the sage or self-realized one who lives at the center point of Tao. Once we identify with the center point, we are truly in harmony with everything.

How can we know how to discern true sages or teachers when we meet them? First, they will be humble about their spiritual achievement, not boastful. They will smile readily and laugh often. They will look us in the eye when they speak with us. They will not claim to be an "expert" in their field. They will not demand to be worshipped as a "saint."

In fact, they will not claim to be enlightened. They will be healthy. They will communicate in a simple and clear way. They will not charge overmuch for their books, courses, or teachings. They will not develop unhealthy relationships with their students. Lastly, they will be seen as continuing with their own cultivation practices.

Ho Shang Kung tells us that "sincere words are true words" but that the one who speaks untrue words "creates sorrow by means of his tongue."[2] He goes on to say that the scholar, or the one who has book knowledge, "sees and hears much, but as he is ignorant, he loses what is important and true."[3]

Here we are at the last step on our journey, yet in truth, this journey has no end. This journey will last us the rest of our life, if not longer. All the advice and practices that we have learned will enrich and illuminate our lives in ways that will take years to truly comprehend. Our journey, like all true journeys, has been a return home. It is the return from complexity to simplicity. It is the unraveling of the ties that bind us. It is the freeing of our souls to wander where there are no roads, yet where every road leads home.

THE PRACTICE   Small Heavenly Orbit

This last practice is an ancient one, called the Small Heavenly Orbit (*xiao zhou tian*) or Lesser Celestial Circuit. This exercise is designed to open our major chi channels and allow our chi to flow more clearly and strongly, leading to a state of inner peace and transformation. This practice is also used to restore universal order within ourselves to regain unity with Tao.

This practice is designed to begin the process of transforming the mundane or Earthly energy of jing to the more pure energy of chi. It is also called "returning the essence to replenish the brain." This is the beginning of the process of transforming the chi into spirit (shen) and then shen into emptiness, or wuji.

When we are in the womb, we are breathing through our belly (dantian), and our du mai channel (up the back) and ren mai channel (down the front) are connected. But when we leave the womb, the channels disconnect. This practice, as with many Taoist practices, is a way to restore that original connection.

The du mai and the ren mai can be thought of as the major highways of the chi system. These two, along with the chong mai (central channel), contain the biggest flow of chi in our body. Yet, like major highways in the world, they can be overcrowded and stuck, with chi backed up like major car traffic. This will cause our chi to move in a tight and sluggish way and can cause many health problems, from slight to serious.

We need to get those highways moving again by guiding the chi along with our mind and breath, so that traffic can move with freedom and speed. There is an old saying in chi gong that says, "Use the mind (yi) to move the chi" or "Chi flows where the mind goes." This practice uses this principle of mind-intent to affect real change in our body—physically and spiritually.

The du mai, which runs up our back, is yang, while the ren mai, which runs down our front, is yin. A blockage or stagnation in either of these two channels will cause an imbalance in our yin/yang energy, which can also cause all kinds of problems.

When doing this practice, it is especially important to touch the tip of your tongue to the roof of your mouth, as you have been doing in your other practices. This will link up the du mai and ren mai, completing the circuit.

- Begin by sitting in stillness, your breath coming and going, like a door opening and closing.

- Put your mind-intent (yi) into your lower dantian.

- Breathe slowly and deeply and feel your "field of elixir" become full of chi.

- Slowly and gently, guide this chi down across your perineum (*hui yin*) and up through your lower back, all the way up to your bai hui point, at the top of your head.

- Remember to do this very gently; it is very important that you do not try to force anything to happen. Forcing is against wu wei and can cause energetic problems.

- In fact, some teachers say not to attempt to guide the energy at all, but just relax deeply and use the mind-intent to open the way so that the chi can move naturally, in its own way.

- There are nine major points along the back and the front of your body through which the chi needs to move.

- Some of them—such as the *wei lu* point on the tailbone; the *ling tai* or Spiritual Tower point, located between the sixth and seventh thoracic vertebrae, opposite the heart center; and *yu gen* or Jade Pillow at the base of the skull—are all places it can be difficult for the chi to pass through.

- Again, do not force anything to happen; just put your focus on these places as the chi rises up your back.

- Once it has risen to the top of the head, gently guide it down the front of your head, across your upper dantian, and down to the upper palate.

- With the tongue resting on your upper palate acting as a conduit, guide the energy down the front of your body, across your middle dantian, and down into the lower dantian.

- Then, with the next breath or series of breaths, guide the energy across hui yin and up the back and then down the front again.

- Each time, it is important that the energy returns to the lower dantian.

- Again, it is extremely important not to attempt to force anything to happen.

- The ideal way to do this practice is to set your mind-intent, begin to breathe deeply and slowly, gather your chi or lifeforce into your lower dantian, and then let it move from there, slowly, naturally, in its own way and time.

- Often, after doing this practice for some time, you will feel a tingling or a sense of warmth as the chi rises and descends.

- In the beginning, you will be using your imagination to move the chi, but eventually, if you are constant with your practice, you will feel the chi moving on its own.

- To finish, put your mind-intent back into your belly, your lower dantian, and relax into a state of mindfulness and gratitude.

---

1. Solala Towler, *Chuang Tzu: The Inner Chapters* (London: Watkins Publishing, 2010), 99.
2. Eduard Erkes, *Ho-Shang-Kung's Commentary on Lao-Tse* (Zurich: Artibus Asiae Publishers, 1950), 134.
3. Ibid.

Afterword

So here we are at the end of our journey together. I hope it has been a fruitful one for you. In truth, the journey we share is everlasting, with many wonderful experiences along the way.

I wish to thank all the Taoist masters throughout time and history, as well as my own teachers, for their guidance and inspiration. I have been on this particular path for over twenty-five years now and am just as excited and inspired by it now as when I first set out.

I hope I have been able to share some of that excitement and inspiration with you, dear readers. I have endeavored to offer, to the best of my limited abilities, a taste of what I have learned and experienced on my own journey.

May your path be strewn with flowers, your journey be full of surprises and delight, your cultivation practices take you to amazing and challenging places, and your way upon the Way be one of joy and fulfillment.

Acknowledgments

Thanks to my publisher, Sounds True—a group of lovely and amazing people who I look forward to traveling with for years to come.

Special thanks to Jennifer Brown, who saw the value of this project, and to my editors—Jennifer Holder, who made editing my book a spiritual retreat and practice of wu wei, and Alice Peck, who jumped in and brought it to completion. Thanks also to my partner, Shanti, for looking over the whole thing at the end.

It really does take many hands to produce a book like this, and I am grateful for every one of them!

About the Author

Solala Towler has taught and practiced Taoist meditation and qigong for more than twenty-five years and is the author of twelve books on the Taoist arts. He is the editor of *The Empty Vessel*, a widely respected journal of Taoist philosophy and practice, published since 1993. He teaches qigong and sound healing at conferences and workshops around the country and leads regular tours to China to study in the sacred Taoist mountains of Wudang. For more information, you can write to him at solala@abodetao.com or visit abodetao.com.

About Sounds True

Sounds True is a multimedia publisher whose mission is to inspire and support personal transformation and spiritual awakening. Founded in 1985 and located in Boulder, Colorado, we work with many of the leading spiritual teachers, thinkers, healers, and visionary artists of our time. We strive with every title to preserve the essential "living wisdom" of the author or artist. It is our goal to create products that not only provide information to a reader or listener, but that also embody the quality of a wisdom transmission.

For those seeking genuine transformation, Sounds True is your trusted partner. At SoundsTrue.com you will find a wealth of free resources to support your journey, including exclusive weekly audio interviews, free downloads, interactive learning tools, and other special savings on all our titles.

To learn more, please visit SoundsTrue.com/freegifts or call us toll-free at 800-333-9185.

SOUNDS TRUE
many voices, one journey